Praise for I I

"*The ancient Greek philosopher Epictetus taught his students that what happens to them is not as important as what they believe happens to them. In this engaging and provocative book, Eldon Taylor provides his readers with specific ways in which their beliefs can lead to success or failure in their life undertakings. Each chapter provides nuggets of wisdom as well as road maps for guiding them toward greater self-understanding, balance, responsibility, and compassion.*"

— **Stanley Krippner, Ph.D.**, Alan Watts Professor of psychology and humanistic studies, Saybrook University, and co-author of *Personal Mythology*

"*I Believe is an inspiring book that shows you all the benefits of choosing your beliefs carefully.*"

— **John Gray, Ph.D.**, *New York Times* best-selling author of *Men Are from Mars, Women Are from Venus*

"*A new view of mind and consciousness is arising from within science and psychology. This emerging picture honors the power of belief, meaning, and purpose, and brings with it stunning possibilities of human potential. Eldon Taylor's I Believe is a no-nonsense invitation to experience this domain for yourself. This book deserves a wide readership, especially for anyone who's interested in self-responsibility and prevention in health. In the end, it's this vision that will turn around our nation's faltering health care, which makes this book all the more important.*"

— **Larry Dossey, M.D.**, author of *Reinventing Medicine* and *The Power of Premonitions*

"*In straightforward Eldon fashion, you'll learn how to plug into all you desire, and you'll understand why you may have been the source of your sabotage. Whether it's a matter of relationships or wellness, prosperity or self-satisfaction, this book will open a new vista of understanding solidly connected to scientific evidence. You'll read it and re-read it, sharing its valuable content with everyone you love.*"

— **Peggy McColl**, *New York Times* best-selling author of *Your Destiny Switch*

"Eldon Taylor's book demonstrates that what we believe directly influences our health, our sense of well-being, and even our aging process. He provides information that will help readers to monitor and shape their own thoughts in ways that may potentially change the readers' lives. The power of our minds shouldn't be underestimated."

— **Chris Carter,** author of *Parapsychology and the Skeptics* and *Science and the Near-Death Experience*

"Eldon's latest book, I Believe, is a study in practical wisdom. He takes generally accepted ideas and turns them inside out so that we can examine our own beliefs in a new and fresh way. I'm reminded of what a late Native American teacher once said: 'If your philosophy doesn't grow corn, I'm not interested.' Eldon's philosophy definitely grows corn. I Believe not only can enrich our lives but also teach us to fully embrace our humanity."

— **Peter Calhoun,** author of *Soul on Fire: A Transformational Journey from Priest to Shaman*

"As the age of unity consciousness is in sight (thank the goddess, I was getting really bored with duality), Eldon throws a huge firecracker into the sky to rain down on us. Absorbing his words is always enlightening, but this time, something's different. In this wonderful book, I Believe, Eldon's tone is softer and more heart-led than usual. Eldon connects the dots, revealing that the divine path is easy when in service to another. Why? Because that's how unity consciousness can start. Connection to others is what helps us reveal our divinity, and from there, we get to live the life we were destined to. We can start the process by accepting our whole self, as we can't connect fully to others if we haven't connected fully to ourselves. That allows the divine being within to shine! Thank you, Eldon. You are one mega connector in our world, and I'm so grateful for the love you poured into this book!"

— **Shazzie,** TV presenter, CEO, and author of *Detox Your World*

"With I Believe, Eldon Taylor has given us another fabulous resource for understanding the power of thoughts and beliefs. He's a master 'sense-maker,' transforming lofty metaphysical concepts into something we can apply and use in our everyday lives."

— **Pam Holloway,** author of *The Credibility Advantage* and *Axis of Influence*

"*Eldon Taylor has done it again with his latest insightful tome. I Believe expands humanity's understanding of what it believes. The book teaches us that 'Our beliefs rule our world' is a more correct thing to say than that intention rules our world. You won't think of yourself the same way after reading I Believe. Perhaps philosopher René Descartes' famous phrase, 'I think, therefore I am,' should also be interpreted, 'When I believe what I think, therefore, that is what I am.'*"

— **Bill Sweet**, past president of Spindrift Research and author of *A Journey into Prayer*

"*An epic, all-encompassing, philosophical masterpiece! Though a deeply personal revelation of the full wealth of one man's life experience, I Believe touches on subject matter deeply significant to all. Never assuming his reader needs yet another 'how to' book, Eldon Taylor shares his wisdom in such a fashion as to gently reawaken the master within each individual. Taylor has Yoda-ized us once again!*"

— **Angelina Heart**, author, teacher, researcher, and facilitator of the Twin Flame information

"*In encountering life's adversities, we often experience fear, doubt, conflict, anxiety, and despair. We stumble, we struggle, we stagger, we suffer, and we sometimes surrender. It often seems like our hopes will go unrealized and our ambitions unattained. Yet we stand up, we settle down, we strive, we surmount, and hopefully, in the end, we soar. With much insight, Eldon Taylor takes us down life's twisting and treacherous path, closely examining the focus and resolve required to help us move from surrendering to soaring.*"

— **Michael Tymn**, author of *The Afterlife Revealed* and *Running on Third Wind*

"*We are, quite simply, products of our belief system. Eldon Taylor's new book I Believe shows how the beliefs that we choose affect our outer world, our health, and our well-being on every level. This prolific author lives what he believes—a successful, fulfilled life. Success is there for all of us when we change our beliefs.*"

— **Caroline Sutherland**, best-selling author of *The Body Knows . . . How to Stay Young*

"At this time in history, when many of us feel humanity is at a crossroads to transformation into the next evolution of consciousness, Eldon Taylor hits the issue on the head with his newest book, <u>I Believe: When What You Believe Matters!</u> It carries on his life's work in helping individuals find their way to their highest potentials, letting go of fear and holding the balance that transforms us so that we, together, can change the world. Created in the image of the Creator, with so much potential in everyone of us, Eldon Taylor reminds us of what we are and where we can go and provides the practical tools that so many need now. This is a wonderful book and road map for reaching our very best."

— **Dr. Nick Begich**, author of *Controlling the Human Mind* and *Earth Rising*

"I love Eldon's perspective of forgiveness and letting go. When we truly forgive, we dispel fear! So forgiveness is actually a powerful tool that we have the agency to use throughout life. . . . I've learned from Eldon's book that when we're quick to forgive— and it becomes a way of life to just 'let go' of circumstances that in the past would have bothered us or caused us to freeze up with anxiety— we find that we have complete and total objectivity in any situation. The natural consequence to this is the dispelling of fear completely out of our lives in all relationships, circumstances, and events. There are no more unspoken agreements or contracts in relationships, no more expectations of others. Instead, there's a complete and total balance of objectivity, a real experience of peace and happiness. The first real step to accomplishing all of this is truly letting go, forgiving, and believing in yourself."

— **Kimberly Gingras**, Mrs. Montana International 2011

"Insightful, profound perspective on human behavior and the beliefs that shape our lives."

— **Elaine Smitha**, author of *Screwing Mother Nature for Profit* and *If You Make the Rules, How Come You're Not Boss?*

"Simply fantastic! As I read Eldon Taylor's <u>I Believe,</u> I kept wondering how Eldon was able to take the 'golden nuggets' of wisdom that I've collected over my lifetime through books, courses, workshops, and personal training and distill them so elegantly into a single volume. Those already deeply into spiritual development and introspective inquiry will truly appreciate what a gem this book is, not only because of the wisdom within its pages but also because of how Eldon brilliantly weaves stories, history, and science together in order to gently invite the reader into a new state of awareness. Another masterpiece by Eldon Taylor!"

— **Karen Kan, M.D.**, law of attraction relationship author and coach

I BELIEVE

ALSO BY ELDON TAYLOR

Plus hundreds of audio and video programs in multiple languages

*Available from Hay House

Please visit:

Hay House USA: www.hayhouse.com®
Hay House Australia: www.hayhouse.com.au
Hay House UK: www.hayhouse.co.uk
Hay House South Africa: www.hayhouse.co.za
Hay House India: www.hayhouse.co.in

I BELIEVE

WHEN WHAT YOU BELIEVE MATTERS!

ELDON TAYLOR

HAY HOUSE, INC.
Carlsbad, California • New York City
London • Sydney • Johannesburg
Vancouver • Hong Kong • New Delhi

Published and distributed in the United States by: Hay House, Inc.: www.hay house.com® • *Published and distributed in Australia by:* Hay House Australia Pty. Ltd.: www.hayhouse.com.au • *Published and distributed in the United Kingdom by:* Hay House UK, Ltd.: www.hayhouse.co.uk • *Published and distributed in the Republic of South Africa by:* Hay House SA (Pty), Ltd.: www.hayhouse.co.za • *Distributed in Canada by:* Raincoast: www.raincoast.com • *Published in India by:* Hay House Publishers India: www.hayhouse.co.in

Cover design: Thebookdesigners • *Front-cover illustration:* Claire Ultimo
Interior design: Tricia Breidenthal

Library of Congress Cataloging-in-Publication Data

Taylor, Eldon.
I believe : when what you believe matters! / Eldon Taylor. -- 1st ed.
    p. cm.
ISBN 978-1-4019-3127-8 (hbk. : alk. paper)
    1. Conduct of life. 2. Belief and doubt. 3. Self-perception. 4.
Self-realization. 5. Self-actualization (Psychology) 6. Success. I.
Title.
BF637.C5T39 2012
155.2--dc23
                2011036261

Tradepaper ISBN: 978-1-4019-3128-5
Digital ISBN: 978-1-4019-3129-2

16 15 14 13   5 4 3 2
1st edition, March 2012
2nd edition, April 2013

Printed in the United States of America

*A wonderful song tells the tale of how the
singers/heroes owe everything to those who are
behind them—those who provided the unseen support,
who continually assured them that they were worthy,
and who had total confidence in them and in their
work. The praise really goes to those who are behind
the scenes—those who are the "Wind beneath
My Wings," as stated in the title of the song
written by Jeff Silbar and Larry Henley.
The wind beneath <u>my</u> wings has been provided
by three people more than all others, and to those
three people I dedicate this work, for without them,
<u>I Believe</u> would not be. To Ravinder, Roy, and Lois—
you have my eternal gratitude! And . . . to my dear
friend and editor of 30 years, Suzanne Brady—
when you stop editing, I stop writing!
Love and Light forever,
Eldon*

CONTENTS

FOREWORD

by Ravinder Taylor

Imagine you could make a choice today that would forever change your life, that would take you from a humdrum, ant-colony-type existence into one where there was no end to the potential that you could express, one that brought a *joie de vivre* to your everyday routines and an assurance that you're firmly on the path toward discovering the answer to the age-old question: *Who am I?* Well, imagine no more, because you're holding the book that can show you definitively the choices you can make to do exactly that.

My name is Ravinder, and I have the amazing good fortune of being married to Eldon and of having him as my very best friend. I met Eldon more than 21 years ago when he was teaching at the National College of Hypnosis and Psychotherapy in England. I was studying at this school because I'd become intrigued by the power of the mind, and I was interested in exploring how far it could extend. Also, although I was still in my 20s, I was already aware that there was much more to this existence than was apparent in the rat race of our daily routines.

I learned a lot from Eldon's first presentation, but one of the most remarkable things related to general health and well-being. At that time, I was, like most people, prone to the seasonal bouts of cold and flu, with the transitions to spring and fall bringing a near-guarantee of another bout of the "snuffles." However, there was something about Eldon's lecture—the scientific facts he presented, real-life testimonials that his readers had shared with him, and his own way of seeing a global picture when most other people saw only a number of random dots—that made a deep impression on me. In a classroom setting, he taught me that I had power over my own state of health. As a result, it was a good ten years before I experienced any kind of ill health again.

So how could one simple lecture give me a decade-long immunity to colds and flu? Well, the answer to that question can be found in the subtitle to this incredible book: *When What You Believe Matters!*

Eldon began teaching about the power of the mind almost 30 years ago. Some of his ideas were way before their time, and it has been interesting to see concepts that he presented back then finally achieving widespread acceptance today. His last four books, all published by Hay House, have highlighted different aspects of the same issue: the disconcerting fact that while the mind is the portal to discovering the higher meaning and purpose of our lives, it's also dreadfully neglected. This is why most of us feel dissatisfied with our lives, experience failures more often than success, find ourselves behaving in ways that are contrary to our best interest, and may be slipping deeper and deeper into a quagmire that we don't know how to escape from.

By looking at the same issue from five different angles—one for each previous book, plus this one—Eldon makes it impossible to ignore the truth behind our day-to-day lives and shows us how we can break free and self-actualize. In *Choices and Illusions,* he highlights the simple fact that while we believe we're in charge of our own thoughts and choices, the reality is very different. In *Mind Programming,* Eldon shows us the organic and planned manipulations of our awareness that occur on a daily basis, and he explains why the vast majority of us simply allow this to happen. *What Does That Mean?* shows us how often we ignore those miraculous events that happen to all of us at some time or another, simply because they defy scientific explanation—and how this is an act of self-betrayal. The fourth volume, *What If?,* has to be one of Eldon's most controversial books, because rather than just explaining how mental manipulation occurs, he goes right into our minds, dissecting our beliefs and desires, and showing how two opposing views can be held at the same time without conscious awareness. Seeing ourselves in the mirror, with nowhere to hide, is a daunting experience for most of us, but this process really is vital if we have any desire or need to discover the real self.

And now, Eldon has brought us a fresh perspective in this amazing new book. Using examples from health to relationships, from goals to intuition, from flaws to enlightenment, and drawing on the latest scientific findings, he shows you how important it is to choose your beliefs and the effects these choices have on your life experience. Plus, you'll discover how easy it is to release new strength from within and open up a vista of possibilities.

As I said earlier, I'm most fortunate in being Eldon's wife and friend. There's nothing I enjoy more than our daily meetings at the dining-room table, where we share a cup of tea and incredible conversations. *I Believe* is an important element in all of these discussions, which have me firmly on the path to reaching my highest aspirations, and I'm thrilled to be able to share this with you. Your reading *I Believe* is like *having you* join in those conversations.

My advice to you is this: Bring an open mind, read carefully, and take the time after each chapter to fully reflect on the information and decide how to incorporate it into your daily life. I promise you that this investment will pay you back time and time again. I know, because I've done precisely that.

This moment is the beginning of a whole new journey for you. Enjoy!

INTRODUCTION

I've written many books on the mind, the manipulators, their tools, and your defenses. I've also written about the psychology of being human, how we make choices, why we choose what we do, and where our self-limiting and self-defeating beliefs originate. If you've read my earlier books, then you recognize that it's not always possible to be uplifting and illuminating while dealing with much of this subject matter. It's because honest introspection is seldom only inspirational that I've chosen to write this book.

I think about all the mechanics behind how the mind works—how it can be duped to confuse us; to lose the authentic self; to destroy our hopes, beliefs, and ambitions—and I feel compelled to answer the question put to me by so many who have read my books, attended my lectures, or listened to my radio broadcasts. They ask: "How do we know ourselves, learn to believe in ourselves, build character, and self-actualize in a world full of agendas, propaganda, and deceit?" I've heard it said that people with character are like planets—they carry their weight and atmospheres along with them wherever their orbit may take them. Character is a hallmark of belief in one's self.

This is a book about what I believe, but it's also something more. It's about something we can all hold true, for it's all about faith in yourself. "When believing in yourself matters" is a slogan I've used for many years. Indeed, I close my radio show with the same statement at the end of every broadcast: "Remember, believing in yourself always matters!" Over the years it has become clear to me that this is all-important, and so I've used it as the subtitle to this book: "When What You Believe Matters!"

How do we build the confidence to be certain that we do, indeed, believe in ourselves? This can be done by examining our lives through a different lens, adjusting our perception, understanding that we're not alone and that others have gone before us, knowing that the fears we might experience have all been vanquished by mere mortals such as ourselves, and being aware that there's no such thing as a law of limitation other than the one we impose upon ourselves. By examining the elements of character—what it means to be a "good" or honorable person—by looking from the outside in, as if through the eyes of another, we can systematically gain the confidence we seek. Every chapter in this book therefore is a near stand-alone treatise on some subject important to character and offers reflections, inviting you not only to consider what has been said but to participate in it. You may do this however you wish: by contemplation, meditation, dream petitioning, journal writing, or whatever other method you prefer. The important thing is for you to take the time to analyze what you currently believe, see if it works for you, and if necessary choose the beliefs that you wish to make your own.

To that end, I welcome you on a journey that may have you weeping at times and laughing at others, but it is a journey that I truly hope leads you to a brighter future, full of possibilities and dreams, the likes of which you may never before have imagined. For, you see, you are a miracle, and you deserve to express the unlimited potential that resides within you.

CHAPTER 1

THE POWER OF BELIEF: WHO AM I?

"The power of belief, the absolutely awesome
incredible power of belief, is the genie in your life.
Let me say that again: The absolutely awesome and
incredible power of your belief is the genie in your life."
— ELDON TAYLOR

One of my favorite writers, Og Mandino, wrote:

One of the painful prices we are paying for our so-called modern lifestyle in the final quarter of this twentieth century is that we are all becoming more and more alike. We all suffer through the same television shows, read the same magazines, wear the same fashions, and buy the same new frozen foods. We all live, and die, by the clock, cut each other off in similar-looking automobiles, pass up a night at the ballgame for a night at the office, never seem to have much time for our spouses or kids, watch helplessly as our oceans and lakes are poisoned, and try not to think of a hydrogen bomb landing anywhere near our city or town.

"We are all, as the years pass, falling in step in order to march to the beat of the *same* drummer, racing forward or backward at the same pace as all others, smiling almost on command—mass-produced beings with no more individuality than any of the millions of saltine crackers that emerge daily from the ovens of Nabisco.[1]

As a student of the mind and human nature, I'm very aware of the role belief has in determining the direct delimiting of that undefined perspective we call "potential." Now juxtapose this with Mandino's observation. What is the real human potential? What is yours? I ask myself all the time, *Who am I?*

The Nearly Unlimited Influence of Belief

DNA

What would you say if I told you that belief influences almost everything in your life, from your DNA[2] to the operation of your endocrine and immune systems, from your emotional well-being to the stability of your moods and attitudes, from your relationships with others to your relationship with yourself—in short, literally every aspect of life? Let me explore that question and in the process share some facts with you.

Levitation

Would it surprise you to learn that belief influences the physical properties in the universe and how you interact with them? How do you think full-body levitation occurs? There is ample evidence that levitation has occurred often in the past and continues to do so today. Indeed, there was a time that levitation was treated as witchcraft.[3] There is also a histor of saints and levitation in both Christianity and Islam, and usually it has been accompanied by a luminous glow around the body. Some of the levitating saints have included Teresa of Avila and Joseph of Cupertino (Friar Giuseppe Desa).[4] Is it possible that levitation was more common back then due to the fact that the masses had not yet learned about the law of gravity?

Placebos and Cures

Thinking, or belief, directly influences the human body. The physical effects of placebos are just one piece of evidence for this claim. It's well known that placebos have healed such incurable health conditions as terminal cancer.[5] In one case, orange-size tumors that filled a man's upper body disappeared when he was given a so-called cure. In a matter of three days, this patient went from gasping for every breath to bouncing around his hospital room, teasing the nursing staff.[6]

Faith Healing

There are many documented reports of miraculous recoveries at the hands of faith healers. Are they further examples of the power of the mind/belief/consciousness? One such miracle worker has been visited by thousands of people from around the world who were previously diagnosed as terminally ill and have come away healed. This miracle worker is João Teixeira de Faria, the man the people of Brazil affectionately call "João de Deus" or "John of God." Qualified professional medical experts have witnessed many of these cases, and the cures are documented. Indeed, a quick Google search for *John of God* will give you weeks of reading material. Do you have to believe to be healed?

Hypnosis

For years I practiced criminalistics, specializing in lie detection and forensic hypnosis. To be certain that I was skilled in the latter, I attended almost every hypnosis school there was. This work paid off when I qualified as an expert in hypnosis during testimony in a murder case. The reason I inject this little bit of history here is to point out that I can credibly affirm that belief has a tremendous amount to do with what individuals can and will experience in hypnosis. I've had clients who didn't believe they could be hypnotized, but by building up their expectations, I've made them very deep hypnotic subjects—by feeding into their understanding, taking them up instead of down, and expanding their consciousness instead of narrowing it. My point here is that *belief* is all-important with respect to outcome.

Once a subject in hypnosis goes deep enough, all kinds of spectacular effects can be produced. Hypnoanalgesia (reduced pain sensitivity) is used as a common antidote for back pain and natural birthing. Indeed, I used hypnosis for a friend of mine while she was giving birth to her first child, and that session lasted more than eight hours.

I once saw Professor Carl LaPrecht put himself in a full-body catalepsy during a training session for lie-detection examiners. Two police officers who were attending the class lifted him up, resting his head on the back of one chair and his heels on the back of another. There he was, wide-eyed and still lecturing—his entire body stiff like a bar of steel. Then he had an officer sit on his belly, and still he remained rigid, in spite of supporting that weight.

Professor LaPrecht was a tall, thin man, not a bodybuilder. What he'd managed to do, using his own self-hypnosis procedure, resembled the stories told about a frantic mother who can lift an automobile off her trapped child. Is this an example of something superhuman or just the result of adrenaline? Either way, a suspension of disbelief must happen. The mother isn't thinking, *I can't do this.* You and I, in the face of solid evidence and firsthand testimony by witnesses, aren't thinking, *That can't be done.* No, we're more likely asking ourselves, *How is this possible?*

I remember as a boy learning about the little engine that could. "I think I can, I think I can, I think I can," it said as it climbed the steep hill, pulling an impossible load. Imagine this same story and its outcome if the train had been saying, "There ain't no way—I can't do this, there ain't no way—I can't do this, there ain't no way—I can't do this." The outcome would most likely have been failure.

Mind-Slaying Effects of Belief

Our beliefs can also deliver the strangest of maladies to our bodies, complete with all the physical symptoms. Indeed, in some instances of mass hysteria, a group of people have been known to fall ill with the same symptoms, such as a rash, high temperature, or abnormal blood counts. In one such instance of mass psychogenic illness, several people reported symptoms that included dizziness, muscle cramps, tremors, and shortness of breath. This occurred in Beirut at a time when the city was under near constant threat of violence, and the case was reported to the Saint George Hospital University Medical Center, where the attending health-care professionals finally diagnosed the problem as "mass psychogenic illness (epidemic sociogenic attacks)."[7]

What about this? Did you know that there are documented multiple-personality cases in which the subject has normal blood sugar in one personality, and the instant another personality takes over, the subject will test hypoglycemic? Now, if that isn't enough to ponder, consider this: There are cases in which eye color changes with the personality, and ones in which extreme allergies come and go with the switches. In fact, according to Michael Talbot in *The Holographic Universe,* it's even more bizarre:

> Each [personality] has his own name, age, memories, and abilities. Often each also has his own style of handwriting, announced gender, cultural and racial background, artistic talents, foreign language fluency, and IQ. . . .
>
> Allergies are not the only thing multiples can switch on and off. If there was any doubt as to the control the unconscious mind has over drug effects, it is banished by the pharmacological wizardry of the multiple. By changing personalities, a multiple who is drunk can instantly become sober. Different personalities also respond differently to different drugs. . . .
>
> There are accounts of epilepsy coming and going with changes in personality, and psychologist Robert A. Phillips, Jr. reports that even tumors can appear and disappear (although he does not specify what kind of tumors).[8]

Mind Influences Machines

Would it surprise you to learn that the power of your intention, what you think, has a well-studied influence on random-number and random-event generators (also known as REGs) and that many such studies have passed peer-review tests before appearing in refereed journals? According to Dean Radin's *Entangled Minds,* the calculated odds that the effects observed in these studies were random or chance are 1 in 10^{76} (1 followed by 76 zeros).[9] Thoughts influence machines!

The Princeton Engineering Anomalies Research (PEAR) program tracked REGs situated around the world, investigating the impact of global consciousness on matter. Princeton University's School of Engineering and Applied Science kept this project going for three decades. Their website states:

> PEAR has now incorporated its present and future operations into the broader venue of the International Consciousness Research Laboratories (ICRL), a 501(c)(3) not-for-profit organization, in addition to Psyleron—a company that provides REG/

RNG devices to enable the continued exploration of PEAR's findings by the general public and research communities.

What were their findings? Summarizing this innovative research can be done simply, although the work itself is far from simple—mind/consciousness does influence the physical world! I quote the PEAR website again:

> Our ability to acquire, or to generate tangible, measurable information independent of distance or time challenges the foundation of any reductionist brain-based model of consciousness that may be invoked. The lack of notable correlations in the data with standard learning curves or other recognizable cognitive patterns, combined with the repeatable and distinct gender-related differences, suggest that these abilities may stem from a more fundamental source than heretofore suspected.[10]

Mind at a Distance

Ingo Swann, an acquaintance of mine and a remote-viewing expert, cited my work in his marvelous book *Your Nostradamus Factor.* Swann is definitely among the most important of all those who have influenced the appreciation and potential of mind power in the past century. His work with the Stanford Research Institute in California, particularly with researchers Russell Targ and Harold Puthoff, as chronicled in their book *Mind-Reach,* initiated a multimillion-dollar government project that lasted years, investigating the influence of mind on matter and the possibilities of employing remote viewing as a spy tool. What Swann was able to do in both of these areas is well documented. Among his most impressive abilities were influencing a magnetometer and viewing distant locations, accurately reporting events as they happened.[11]

The magnetometer feat was quite remarkable. To truly grasp this, allow me to quote from the *Science of the Lost Symbol:*

> What's a magnetometer? Basically, it's a device that detects and measures the magnetic field. In this case, one of Puthoff's post-doctoral students had devised a type of magnetometer

impressively called a superconducting quantum interference device (SQUID for short) that was able to screen out the strong vibrations from most common fields, such as the electromagnetic field, to detect only the tiniest vibrations of subatomic particles. Swann faced a formidable challenge, for the magnetometer's internal parts were shielded in alternating layers of aluminum, copper, nobium[sic], and other metals to block electromagnetic and other kinds of fields, and it was then encased in concrete five feet below the lab floor. There was no way for Swann to actually see or interact with the device.

As we said, Swann's task was to alter the output of the magnetometer using only his mind. Normal output was represented graphically as a sine wave, a regularly undulating S-curve. Any change in its detection of the magnetic field would show up on the output graph as a change in the S-curve, usually as a flat line.

Swann was wildly successful at affecting the output of the machine. Puthoff was mystified, and he put Swann through a series of exercises, cueing him to direct his attention to the machine for a specific amount of time, then not to focus, then to focus again. When Swann focused his attention on changing the output of the machine, the S-curve flattened out.

Then Swann really blew Puthoff's mind. He said he was going to project his mind into the machine to see what its insides were like, so he might be even more effective at changing its output. Soon he was intently drawing a picture of what he saw inside the machine, including a nobium[sic] ball at its center. Illustrations of the inside of the machine had never been published, so Puthoff showed the drawing to the post-doc who had constructed the machine. He verified that Swann's drawing was accurate.[12]

As for the remote viewing, the late Lynn Schroeder and her partner, Sheila Ostrander, both friends of mine, reported in *Psychic Discoveries behind the Iron Curtain* that the Russians were working on this phenomenon long before the U.S. government decided to play catch-up with their remote viewing project called *Grill Flame/ Star Gate*.[13]

Consciousness Influences Plants

Consciousness has also been shown to influence plants. One of my favorite experiments for showing young people this phenomenon has to do with how our mental state, specifically our emotion—and to be clear, there's no such thing as human emotion unaccompanied by a mental state—influences plant growth. The experiment goes like this: Take two normal beans from the bag in your pantry, and plant them in identical soil and pots. Place them side by side on the same window ledge. Name one of them "Ugly" and the other "Love." Every day for 30 days, take them from the window ledge and praise Love with glowing remarks about how beautiful it is and how much you love it—and be sincere. Then take Ugly and tell it just how much you detest it, how you wish it would die, how it is the manifestation of everything wrong and ugly in the world. Vent (or invent) all the hostile feelings of absolute contempt that you can muster and dump them on Ugly. In 30 days, you will see a distinct difference between the two plants.

Cleve Backster, a fellow former lie-detection examiner, showed not only that plants respond to human consciousness and actions but also that they have memory.[14] Backster was one of the pioneers of bio-communication, the study of communication between different life forms. Even though the Discovery Channel television show *MythBusters* failed to replicate Backster's work, his contributions have far-reaching consequences. (On the radio show *Coast to Coast AM,* hosted by George Noory, Backster discredited *MythBusters* on the basis of their experimental design.)

Backster claimed to be able to measure the influence of consciousness on white blood cells, eggs, and yogurt cultures. Harold E. Puthoff and Randall Fontes at Stanford Research Institute published a paper that supports Backster's view of consciousness in a report called "Organic Biofield Sensor."[15]

Randall Fontes's career path was largely set by his graduate project, in which he sought to research the action potential in the algae *Nitella* to determine sensitivity to various external stimuli.

His conclusions clearly demonstrate a reaction, or exchange of some kind, that takes place between plant and human consciousness. His research was highlighted in the best-selling book *The Secret Life of Plants,* by Peter Tompkins and Christopher Bird.

Consciousness Influences the Elements

There's prolific anecdotal evidence that consciousness influences phenomena such as wind, rain, and storms. Shamans claim to be able to speak with nature and often affect animals as well. I personally know one such individual, Peter Calhoun, who appears to have at least some control over earth, wind, water, and fire. He has, in full view of numerous witnesses, called up storms and filled the sky with clouds. Was the weather a coincidence? Peter is a former Episcopal priest who, together with his wife, Astrid, teaches shamanism in remote areas of America. In a vision, Peter was told that we're all individual manifestations of an Infinite Creator—beings without limitations of any kind! Could the teachings of shamans, druids, and others actually have a place in our modern, scientific world?

I am a scientist. I hold a graduate degree that says so, and I have patents that also support this claim. I've conducted research myself and participated in designing numerous other experiments. I'm listed in *Who's Who in Science and Engineering,* so I think I can call myself a scientist with some certainty. I've also always had an affinity with nature. I believe animals sometimes understand our intentions more clearly than we do ourselves, and I think that nature is sensitive to the consciousness of all living things. Why? Let me share a story with you, and you decide if it was just coincidence or something more.

In 1996, I felt prompted to speak to my wife about the trees on our small horse ranch. We have several hundred trees, mostly pines. I make it a habit to recognize them, to thank them for protecting us from the wind and the burning sun, and for casting an awesome presence over our entire property. My wife, also a scientist (a microbiologist), wasn't so sure about my mental soundness, but she trusted me nevertheless and agreed to speak to the trees as I asked her to. Throughout the entire spring, summer, and fall of that year, we both *hugged* them, if not physically, then verbally.

In November 1996, a major ice storm brought down more than 60 trees, many of them large, mature pines that were 30 to 40 feet tall. Not one of them did any damage to the structures on our property. They broke and fell over fences, but a branch held each one just above the fence, not allowing them even to stretch the wire. One huge tree came down over the birdhouse, which is home to our chickens and pigeons. Again, the tree supported itself with a large branch, thereby preventing itself from crushing the house.

It was truly amazing, and everyone who saw it was flabbergasted by the event. Not a single fence, building, or other possession was damaged. The loss of the trees was difficult, but the phenomenon really tests the idea of coincidence. So where do mind and consciousness really leave off?

Mind to Mind with Animals and Cells

On more than one occasion, I've been blessed to feel that I could communicate with an animal in distress. For example, I was once called to the scene of an accident in which a trailer loaded with two horses had come off the hitch and turned over on the side of the freeway. The horses were trapped inside. This was an extremely dangerous situation. How could they not panic and kick and struggle? God help anyone who got in the middle of it! Nevertheless, I was able to somehow let both animals know that they'd be okay, and I slowly worked them out without incident—no kicking, no panicking, and no injury.

On another occasion, the owners and two would-be trainers of a famous thoroughbred stallion that was boarded at my ranch had managed to upset their horse so much while trying to load him into a trailer that the animal was cut in several places, including above the eye. He was bleeding, snorting, and refusing to move forward into the trailer. When I arrived and saw what was transpiring, I took the stallion from them and led him inside the barn. I washed him, provided first aid, and spoke to him, apologizing for what had happened. Then I walked him right into the trailer. Was this a coincidence?

Many animal trainers insist that they communicate with their subjects, and I believe them. Sometimes this communication is silent—mind to mind, if you will. How can this be? Is it possible if you don't believe it is?

In my book *Wellness: Just a State of Mind?* I reported on how some cells were removed from the body and then divided between two petri dishes. One was taken as many as five miles away from the other, yet when an electrical shock was delivered to one set of cells, the other set responded as though it had just received the direct current. Cell consciousness was communicating at a distance.[16]

Trained meditators control many aspects of their bodily functions. Dr. Herbert Benson of Harvard Medical School has reported on Tibetan monks who can produce enough body heat to dry wet sheets placed on their shoulders in a cold, damp room. According to the *Harvard Gazette*, this type of temperature control is common among trained meditators.[17]

You may also be interested in the demonstrated fact that meditation actually can change brain structure by building stronger connections. Researchers at the University of California–Los Angeles recently reported this finding. They pointed out that stronger connections translate into the ability to relay electrical signals rapidly.[18]

There are many stories about the practitioners of certain spiritual arts doing such things as eating hot coals, chewing glass, and walking on nails. Indeed, in recent years these events have become less spectacular because they've become increasingly common. What anyone will tell you who has ever attended or been a facilitator at one of these shows is that belief makes all the difference. If you believe those coals are going to burn you, they will.

Amazing Brain/Mind Power

One popular notion about the mind that's based on a falsehood—or rather, an urban legend—is often attributed to Albert Einstein. That story argues that we use only about 10 percent of our brain, and therefore the other 90 percent has supreme potential. Well, the initial figure might just as well have been 1 percent or 50 percent, for there's no such real measurement. Most of the brain is used for something.

Nevertheless, this is a powerful metaphor for looking at limitations. Whenever I think about this metaphor, I'm reminded of the many savants who testify to amazing mental abilities. Some can tell you what day of the week your birthday will fall on 50 years from now as fast as you ask the question; some are musical geniuses; others have amazing mathematical talent; still others have amazing linguistic, mechanical, or spatial skills. There are many theories about what underlies these precocious abilities, but what they definitely all share is an uncanny ability to do something considered generally above and beyond the scope of even genius human capability. Take, for example, the mathematical wizard who can calculate elaborate equations faster than a computer—how is that possible? Can each of us find our own inner savant?

What, then, is the limitation of consciousness and the mind, and how much of it is dictated by belief? Could we all have such skills if we only believed that we could? Could we at least train this ability within ourselves if we believed the endeavor would be successful?

Brainwashing

In contrast to all the marvelous potential we might conjure up, there are also many sinister possibilities. In my book *Mind Programming,* I cited the conclusion reached by the U.S. Central Intelligence Agency regarding brainwashing, as reported to Congress by Jules Romains, which stated flatly that a man could be convinced to kill his aged parents and cook them in a stew.[19]

What then is the real power of the mind and the engine that appears to drive its most spectacular possibilities? In a word, *belief!* In my view, this is the ultimate frontier. One day, perhaps we'll have the switch that turns on belief, and we'll be able trigger within ourselves a cure for cancer just as easily as flipping on a light. Or maybe we'll want to experience being lighter than air, so we'll engage yet another switch, and *voilà,* we'll be able to levitate.

The Power of Belief

This is what I hold to be true: belief dictates your life as surely as magnetism directs a compass needle. If you deem yourself unworthy, you'll prove it to be so. If you think you're unfit, you'll find a way to manifest that. I cannot overemphasize both the potential power in our beliefs and the necessity of choosing them wisely.

Unfortunately, most of us haven't consciously chosen most of our beliefs. In my book *What If?* I made the case for examining our life and all that we hold true. As Socrates is credited with saying, "The unexamined life is not worth living." I believe that we have both the prerogative and the obligation to know what we think and why. Those who choose to close their minds, believing that they know all there is to know, that they have the only right way, or that there's no such thing as *blank* (say, miracles), have blinded themselves to experiencing much of the true meaning in life—and of being who they really are.

It's popular in certain circles today to assert that science has all the answers. This claim is interesting, especially when those who make the claim often fail at being true scientists, and they fail by definition, for a scientist is someone who investigates, not someone who closes the mind and refuses to look. *Skeptic* is another word often heard nowadays to describe those who banish the possibility of life being more than just what's currently provable. This, too, is a misnomer, for the word *skeptic* implies an openness to inquiry. History informs us that true skeptics eventually find that nothing is certain, including science. The elusive epistemological certainty simply doesn't exist, except for uncertainty—and that can't be known for sure.

So what is it you believe? Those tenets can empower your life or cripple your every hope and ambition. In the chapters that follow, I'll examine different beliefs and how they might influence our realities. I'm a simple, outcome-oriented guy, so I'll attempt to keep the focus on just that—how our beliefs influence the world we live in and the people we've become.

Reflection

Belief influences everything from DNA molecules to machinery. Choosing your beliefs may therefore be the most important choice you can make. Believing in yourself, your own power and ability, whether to heal yourself or to accomplish your ambitions, always matters!

What beliefs do you have that may be self-limiting, that may have affected your relationships, moods, or well-being? If there are any, do you wish to keep them?

CHAPTER 2

DON'T TAKE YOURSELF TOO SERIOUSLY

*"I would rather live my life as if there is
a God and die to find out there isn't, than live my
life as if there isn't and die to find out there is."*
— ATTRIBUTED TO ALBERT CAMUS

It can be easy to confuse living according to our beliefs with firmness, conviction, and perseverance as being contradictory to living a life of balance and nonattachment. Yet these two ideas are in fact complementary. The foundation for refraining from taking ourselves too seriously is understanding our self-image—the ego.

While visiting San Diego recently, my wife and I went to dinner with my son Taylor, who lives nearby. During dinner, he shared a story with us regarding a Vipassana meditation retreat. He gave me permission to share his story:

> There I sat in deep meditation, feeling as though I were in tune with every cell in my body. I was completing a ten-day course that included ten hours of meditation each of those days. It was the morning of day eight, and I'd passed what I thought were the most difficult two days (days four and five). Those were the toughest for me because I thought my brain was going to divorce itself for making the decision to do something that it found almost unbearable. On those two days, my thoughts were, *What the hell am I doing here? I'm just sitting here doing nothing. Have I lost my mind?* I was starting to think I might go crazy from such a lack of stimuli.
>
> You see, "noble silence" was part of this program. This meant that there was no talking, writing, drawing, or even making eye contact unless it was absolutely necessary. Electronic devices, including cell phones, weren't allowed either. This retreat was located up in the mountains, so most of the time the only sounds were birds and the occasional breeze blowing through the trees. Really, the only noise that wasn't a part of nature came from the bell that rang when it was time to eat. Almost as if we'd been trained by Pavlov himself, the clanging would cause all who heard it to salivate.
>
> As I said, it was day eight, and I was finally feeling great about my decision to be there. *So what's for lunch?* I thought. *Oh brother, I can't believe I did that again. What a lousy mind I have. It can't seem to stay focused even after eight days of this meditation!*

Just then, the bell signaled that it was time for dinner. A grin came over my face. Clearly, I wasn't the only person who was anticipating dinner, as most of us proceeded down the path at a pace that resembled a trot more than a walk.

When I entered the kitchen, I saw a room full of smiles, and it soon became clear why. Lunch was a three-bean soup that was absolutely phenomenal! We all knew this because it was the same soup the staff had served for the previous meals that day. It was also, no doubt, a major contributing factor to my lack of concentration during previous meditation sessions that day.

You see, it wasn't just how great this soup tasted that made my thoughts wander. It was also the effect that eating such a large quantity of beans was having on my digestion. By the time the previous meditation session ended, I was having to lean to either side every five minutes or so to release the built-up pressure in my lower abdomen. It was also becoming apparent from the constant gurgling noises, occasional muffled toots, and even random suppressed giggles coming from all directions that I wasn't the only person affected this way.

After filling our bellies with this delicious soup, we returned to the meditation hall for our last session of the day. By the time most of us had taken our seats on the floor, an older, saintly looking woman entered the room. She looked like a very wise and gentle being and reminded me very much of Mother Teresa. She began to take her seat in the front row. Halfway to the floor, with her bottom stuck in the air, she suddenly farted loudly—and everyone heard.

This was the final straw. Everyone laughed out loud uncontrollably for several seconds. Throughout the rest of that particular meditation session, you could hear random, muffled farting noises followed by outbursts of laughter.

Who says farts aren't funny—even in such a spiritual setting as this?

We are all spirits inhabiting bodies, or so they say. However, it's clear that we're also truly *in* our bodies and, as another trite but true saying puts it, we all put our pants on one leg at a time. Then why is it so easy to take ourselves too seriously?

Annoyances

What is it that we worry about, that we allow to fester and annoy us, that we find unacceptable, and why? I've asked many people about what upsets them, and generally I like to phrase the question along these lines: "Will it make any difference 50 years from now?"

If that doesn't defuse the matter, then I proceed to the next question: "Is it the most important matter in your life, in your relationships, or in your future at this moment?" If that doesn't work, then I ask, "If the worst possible outcome actually transpires, then what?" After the person answers, I continue, "And then what?" And again if needed: "And then what?" Using this method, we eventually come to the point that whatever will be, will be—time for the old *Doris Day Show* and its theme song, "Que Sera, Sera. Whatever Will Be, Will Be."

There's a saying that I think of when my friends treat me differently because I'm a *New York Times* best-selling author: "Never believe your own publicity." I remind myself of that often. Nevertheless, I sometimes find myself becoming annoyed when the service I'm paying for (say, in a restaurant) is so substandard as to be virtually nonexistent or when the stranger on the other end of the phone lied to get me to take the call, wants to sell me something, and acts like a long-lost friend.

When I think about annoyance, I find that I can be easily knocked off balance by someone who shows total disrespect for anything dear to me, including myself. Indeed, I've had the privilege of rubbing elbows with many famous people—writers, actors,

CEOs, and sports figures—and I know of not even one who doesn't expect to be treated with respect, or who can easily dismiss an intentional slight. Should they? What about you? Why should this matter? The truth is, it really doesn't.

So, is there anything we *should* take seriously? What if one of our children is spat upon by a teacher, figuratively speaking—or literally, for that matter? Do we have a right to become serious? If so, where's the line?

The Middle Path

"Let go and let God" is a well-known saying that's part of 12-step recovery programs. What do you believe? When is it your responsibility to act (right action), and when is it wise just to let go?

Spiritual systems generally teach something that mystics refer to as "the middle path," or sometimes "the middle pillar." The idea is that somewhere between the extremes is a place of balance. I think we all seek this balance, and I believe that it's the secret to a life filled with joy and harmony. Do we then disregard matters that are disturbing? Do we just remain unattached? That is, should we do what we can but remain disinterested in the outcome?

To ignore disturbance is to avoid dealing with it, but your conscience still knows what doesn't resonate with the truth as you believe it to be. So what's the higher meaning of detachment? It doesn't mean just writing off other people as if you don't care about them or about what happens. Instead, remain unattached to your own reaction—as in, "Don't take yourself too seriously"— so that you're clear of mental and emotional disturbances. This allows you to access your intuitive power and thus influence the situation by extending your unbiased aid.

In some cases, it may be helpful to be patient and neutral, explaining calmly what it is that's disturbing. At other times, it may be more useful to really yell in order to jolt someone out of his train of thought. Remaining unattached means seeing the situation from the point of view of what's needed in order to lend a hand, not from annoyance, self-righteousness, or ego-centered feelings.

Being attached to whether we've been helpful, whether our advice is respected, or whether the other person agrees or rebukes us is another disturbance to our ego. Everyone is on his or her personal journey, and they all must decide for themselves what their actions will be. For the most part, our duty is simply to point out the alternatives and then let the other people go toward whatever they wish, unless that action endangers others.

It can be very difficult to find the middle path. Extremes in politics, religions, value systems, and economic situations all keep the teeter tottering. To get it balanced, we should do more than just let go and let God or remain unattached to the outcome—or should we? It turns out that the balance mystics refer to isn't about remaking the external world—it's about remaking our own internal world.

Doing Your Best

If I want to be successful, according to all those who have succeeded big, I must be focused, diligent, and willing to persevere—to dedicate myself to a goal, an objective. I must energize my efforts in every way, including through visualization. How does all that fit with letting go?

First, you measure your success by your own yardstick, not by others who have appeared to succeed. Second, striving to do your best isn't contradictory to balance or peace, whether you're cleaning a toilet or winning an event at the Olympics. How is that letting go? Again, you're not ceasing your efforts; you're letting go of your reaction to the outcome. When you've done your best, you're happy. When you're striving to win, then all but the champions are unhappy.

Seeking success as an athlete, as a businessperson, or as anything else requires tenacity, endurance, and confidence. Because of that, you may ask, *Where's the line between detachment, letting go, and creating my own future to the best of my ability?*

There is no line. You remain unattached to false ego-building, not to sincere efforts to do good work. That said, remember not to take yourself too seriously because there can be "fart-ful" moments in the most somber of occasions. If you go with it, you'll laugh and enjoy the experience.

Reflection

As you've seen, it can be easy to confuse living according to your beliefs with firmness, conviction, and perseverance as contradictory to balance and nonattachment. Nevertheless, they are in fact complementary. The foundation for refraining from taking ourselves too seriously is in understanding our self-image—the ego. Have you ever taken yourself too seriously?

CHAPTER 3

BE HONEST WITH YOURSELF AND EMBRACE YOUR FLAWS

"I don't see myself as beautiful, because I can see a lot of flaws. People have really odd opinions. They tell me I'm skinny, as if that's supposed to make me happy."

— ATTRIBUTED TO ANGELINA JOLIE

Flaws are an interesting notion—thinking about them reminds me of the old saying, "One man's junk is another man's treasure." What is a flaw?

For some people, such little things as acne, skin discolorations, or what the Brits call a "ruddy" complexion, are problems. For other people, it's a matter of body weight or fitness. Still others have their eyes fixed on proportions, and we could go on with a very long list of personal preferences. But these are all physical issues. What about speech impediments, low IQ, or learning disabilities—or do we enter this realm at our peril, since so much of this territory is protected by political correctness?

What do we mean by a flaw? Eugenic theorists today might insist that a real defect is the result of two unfit people being allowed to reproduce. We don't talk about it much, but not long ago many "unfit" individuals were unceremoniously and unwillingly sterilized. Most states had laws on the books that prevented "defectives" from adding to the population's gene pool.

In 1924, a supervising health-care professional filed a petition to sterilize Carrie Buck, an 18-year-old reported to have the intelligence of a 9-year-old. It's an interesting case and well worth checking out, but for our purposes, all we need to know is that the intent was to protect the gene pool from flaws. In the famous case of Buck v. Bell, esteemed United States Supreme Court Justice Oliver Wendell Holmes argued that the purity of the gene pool outweighed the interest of the individual:

> We have seen more than once that the public welfare may call upon the best citizens for their lives. It would be strange if it could not call upon those who already sap the strength of the State for these lesser sacrifices, often not felt to be such by those concerned, to prevent our being swamped with incompetence. It is better for all the world, if instead of waiting to execute degenerate offspring for crime, or to let them starve for their imbecility, society can prevent those who are manifestly unfit from continuing their kind. The principle that sustains compulsory vaccination is broad enough to cover cutting the Fallopian tubes.[1]

Yet I have seen some pretty spectacular things from so-called idiots. Indeed, we use the term *savants* today, as mentioned in

Chapter 1, but the original term was *idiot-savant* because where the gift was present—such as a gift with integers—it was specialized. For example, while the savant who specialized in numbers might be able to tell you the day of the week on which you would turn 65 years old, he'd nevertheless typically lack the ability to live on his own or even balance a checkbook, for that matter. In *The Man Who Mistook His Wife for a Hat and Other Clinical Tales,* Oliver Sacks tells the story of the twins he met who could neither perform multiplication nor read, yet played a game of finding very large prime numbers. There are many such cases. Are these oddities to be eliminated or retained only for research purposes, all in the name of flaws—gene-pool flaws?

Eugenics is a subject beyond the scope of this book, though it is one that has moral implications we should all carefully sort through—case by case, in my opinion—so let's just get back to apparent defects. It would seem that there are numerous possibilities, depending on where we look and who's doing the looking; however, not one of them is what I consider to be a fault.

I believe that the only true flaws are those of character. Thomas Paine said, "Character is much easier kept than recovered." This goes hand in hand with integrity, which we'll peer into deeply in the next chapter, but for now I want to focus on the aggregate of beliefs and traits that make for an admirable character.

Webster's dictionary defines character in this sense as "a person marked by notable or conspicuous traits." What, then, is an admirable character for a person?

It has two "legs" upon which it usually stands. The first is integrity (which, as already mentioned, we will discuss in the next chapter). The second is reputation.

Reputation and Character

Reputation follows you—even if you don't think you know what it is. It's essentially how others perceive you. If you think for a moment, you should be able to come up with an idea of what you'd like your reputation to be. Are you affable or stoic in your exchanges? Do others see you as gregarious or introverted? I could go on with various qualities, but these aren't your character—or at least the aspect that's under review at this moment. No, the qualities I want to get to are honesty, trustworthiness, and stability. Can you be counted upon?

Is your character strengthened by your convictions, or is it weakened? Do you stand for anything larger than your self-interest? Are you courageous, and can you be depended upon in an emergency to do your best? Are you patient, generous, caring, empathic, sharing, flexible, forgiving, gentle, grateful, hospitable, and sincere? Are you secure, thorough, thoughtful, compassionate, honorable, loyal, wise, discreet, discerning, and tolerant? What's the list of character traits that you'd like to be perceived as having?

One problem in our society today is the lack of emphasis on virtue and values in our educational system. In my opinion, the strides that have been made over the years to avoid discrimination have all too often created a vacuum in teaching the principles of a moral life. Indeed, the more we've attempted to be inclusive in this way, the more we've moved away from true values. Under this logic, it follows that anything is right if the culture says it is.

I believe that character requires virtue, which has many components, including an absolute value system. I'm not altogether certain how this system should be articulated, but it begins by recognizing the rights of all people to at least their lives, liberty, and the pursuit of happiness. In my book *What If?* I examine the notion of the pursuit of happiness because it can mean different things to different people. In deference to my regular readers, I won't go into detail about that here, but suffice it to say that I believe in absolute values.

What is character for the cultural relativist other than following the crowd, doing as they do without an eye to a higher standard? I suppose we could say they're accepting, allowing, permissive, and flexible. But what would we say about their character if they accepted, for example, the Pakistani government's sentence of execution for a Christian woman, allegedly because she defended her religion, something that filled headlines as recently as 2010? Asia Bibi was sentenced to death for blaspheming Islam.[2]

Pakistan has a blasphemy law that many would say is both ignorant and unjust. In my mind, that law is just another perversion of Muhammad's teachings. But the fact is that for cultural relativists, such a law is okay. Well, maybe they don't personally endorse the situation, but then it's not up to them, is it? That's the usual retort I get when questioning some such individuals in this way.

Character is often the one outstanding lesson in life and fiction. A strong resolve, a high standard, and virtue (which I'll discuss more in the next chapter)—together with such admirable characteristics as forgiveness, gratitude, intelligence, honesty, and trustworthiness—are the ingredients of moral character. But they begin with a value system, as in the statement: "This is what I can say that I believe, and it includes life, liberty, and the pursuit of happiness."

How obvious this seems, especially in the United States. How often this value system is unspecified as the building block of character—again, especially in this great country. It raises this question in my mind: *Is lack of character the real flaw, and whose flaw is it?*

Reflection

So what do you believe? Are there aspects of yourself that you think of as flaws? Are they really defects, or are they just characteristics that define your individuality? What would happen if you stopped seeing them as negative? Would you be happier? And what do you think about your character? Is there any part of it that you'd like to work on? What will it take for you to be the type of person you truly admire? What will you do differently today in order to build in yourself this kind of character?

CHAPTER 4

INTEGRITY INVIOLATE

*"It's not what we eat but what we digest that makes us strong;
not what we gain but what we save that makes us rich; not what
we read but what we remember that makes us learned; and not
what we profess but what we practice that gives us integrity."*

— **ATTRIBUTED TO FRANCIS BACON**

There's a marvelous story told by American businessman Jon
Huntsman regarding a $57-million deal that he made on a hand-
shake. It took the attorneys some six months to get the paper-
work in order; and by the time the contracts were ready, the value
of the company Huntsman was selling had grown to more than
$150 million. However, because he'd given his word, because his

handshake meant something real to him, he honored the deal, even though the buyer himself had offered to compromise. Huntsman's message is well captured in the title of his book: *Winners Never Cheat—Even in Difficult Times.*

When I was young, my mother told me things such as, "Cheaters never win." But when I was young, I saw many cheaters come out on top. They won at card games, they won playing Monopoly, and they even won in some sports events. It seemed to me that those with the "sharp angle" or those sly "fast-hand" artists were always winning.

I understood the intent of my mother's admonition, but what if you didn't have a conscience? What if there were no angels, masters, guides, or for that matter, no heaven and hell? What if the whole notion of a god was but a fictional leftover from the basic animistic instincts of our primitive ancestors? Under these circumstances, cheating could well have its advantages, couldn't it?

With the exception of the sociopath, everyone seems to have what our wise elders have identified as a conscience. Society as a whole becomes more cohesive as a result of our collective acknowledgment of right and wrong. Even in tribal groups, the community sense of conscience organizes the tribe in such a way as to censure incorrect behavior. Researchers differ on how much of that is the result of our environment and how much is innate, but they don't disagree that often this small, internal voice dictates individual sacrifices in foregoing principles of pleasure while enduring units of pain.[1]

What happens when the small voice goes silent for the individual or the culture? There are far too many examples of societies that turn their backs, shut down their conscience, or allow moral urgings to fall on deaf ears. Some examples may be found in the Holocaust; genocide in Bosnia and Herzegovina, Rwanda, Cambodia, and Turkey; Stalin's forced famine in Ukraine; and the action of Japan's Imperial Army when they marched into Nanking and murdered 300,000 out of 600,000 people in the city—and all of this within just the twentieth century.

Compromise

Compromise is often thought of as the best possible solution to otherwise irresolvable differences. When is a compromise good? Is it ever bad? What if Jon Huntsman had compromised? Why not split the difference between what he'd agreed to and what the value of the company had become, as even the buyer suggested? For Jon Huntsman, your word is your word—you don't go back on it. Is this foolish?

Imagine that you're Huntsman. What would you do? The difference is millions of dollars. Would you compromise? *Should* you compromise? When is giving your word meaningful, after all?

The real you—not the person whom others see but the self who knows when your word is good and when it isn't—can be defined by your degree of integrity. Does your true self make your word "golden," as Huntsman's was? Or does the real you measure it according to the circumstances, finding rational ways to justify whatever your decision might be at the time?

I believe that integrity should be inviolate. If you give your word, you keep it. If you shake hands on a deal—that's your promise. I believe that every time you compromise this principle, you prostitute your character. In time, well, it won't much matter who comes along and wants to bed you—it will be all about what's in it for you. This is as true about your values as it is about your word.

I remember the words of Robert Kennedy regarding this:

> Few men are willing to brave the disapproval of their fellows, the censure of their colleagues, the wrath of their society. Moral courage is a rarer commodity than bravery in battle or great intelligence. Yet it is the one essential, vital quality for those who seek to change a world that yields most painfully to change.[2]

Is that what Jon Huntsman is—a morally courageous person? I've spoken to some who insist he was a fool for not renegotiating the deal or at least accepting the buyer's offer. This is a slippery slope, some might say, this idea of *Why not compromise, just once? Why not bend the meaning of "It's a deal" to fit changing circumstances?*

Promises

It's easy for parents to promise their children the sky. What parents haven't found themselves saying such things as these:

- "I'll never leave you."
- "I promised that I'd take you to the movies before you lost your temper and kicked the door, but I'm not taking you now."
- "I said you could have that item before I lost my job."
- "When I told you that, I didn't know about [fill in the blank]."
- "I said you could choose your friends, but that doesn't include [druggies, delinquents, or whomever—again, you fill in the blank]."

Most parents admit to having said something very nearly the same as every one of these statements, and this list doesn't even begin to represent the proverbial tip of the iceberg.

The fact is that most people pass their word around without a thought as to the consequences. We all say things we don't mean, even if we think we're sincere at the moment. It shouldn't surprise us, then, that by doing this we actually lever ourselves in the direction of tilting our meaning to be whatever we see fit, whenever we find it convenient, and so on. By not keeping our word in certain circumstances, we make it easier to accept the same action in others. Do we mean to do that?

A well-known saying attributed to Archimedes is relevant here: "Give me a lever long enough and a fulcrum on which to place it, and I shall move the world." A lever is very powerful, and once we begin to allow the erosion of our word, regardless of the rationalizations we use to justify it, we weaken our resolve by precedent.

The rationalizations used according to the urgency and situation of the moment become the levers we need to justify why we might cheat on our taxes or keep incorrect change when it's in our favor.

Integrity

I was in a grocery store recently with my youngest son, William James Taylor. We went to the ATM to obtain our cash for the groceries, and William pulled out two $20 bills just as my withdrawal was ejecting from the machine. I hadn't seen them, so when he informed me that they weren't part of our withdrawal, we double-checked our counting. Sure enough, we had an extra $40.

William knew that we could use the money—it was Christmastime, and there was a lot of shopping yet to do—but he also knew it wasn't his (or ours). So on his own, he returned the money. We spoke about how easy it would have been to keep that $40, and then we discussed the ramifications of that simple act.

First, we would have compromised our own principles, and once we'd done so, it would be easier to do so the next time. Then, what if the person who'd left the money discovered the shortage and returned to the store? It could be really important. I had William ruminate over this for a while, and soon he was offering many reasons why the money should be returned.

I don't believe you should compromise your integrity. That said, having this ideal and living up to it may not always be possible, if for no other reason than we've often become far too sloppy about when and where we make our commitments. Still, if I think ahead and value my word, then I won't make promises that leave me no way out when there should be one. For example, in the earlier list of statements made to children, the promise could have been: "I'll take you to the movies so long as your behavior and attitude remain positive and pleasurable to be around." With my sons, we have a caveat to all promises, which is that they're all subject to "AB"—attitude and behavior. Nevertheless, I find myself keeping promises only because I gave my word and for no other reason. I believe that's important—do you?

It all comes down to how much you value your integrity. Do you treasure the idea that you'll do your very best today and every day to hold it inviolate? Will you do what you say you will, live up to your promises, measure yourself positively against your own virtues, hold values that demand the highest from you, and be unafraid to show that rarest of all commodities—moral courage?

I believe that honor begins with integrity and that to fail to honor yourself is a certain path to an empty, unfulfilled life. It's the ultimate cheaters game, for you're cheating no one more than yourself!

Plato tells us of four cardinal virtues: wisdom, courage, moderation, and justice.[3] To consciously persist in cultivating these qualities over a lifetime, little by little every day, examining and reexamining our lives, taking every situation individually to find its meaning, if only to ourselves—this is the noble life that leads to becoming a good human being. For me, Shakespeare's statement, "This above all, to thine own self be true," is the litmus test for progress. In other words, if I can't do it perfectly to begin with, then I'll work at it until I get it as close to perfect as I can.

The Story of the Seeds

This delightful story by an unknown author is worth considering at this point:

> A successful businessman was growing old and knew it was time to choose a successor to take over the business. But instead of choosing one of his directors or his children, he decided to do something different. He called together all the young executives in his company.
>
> He said, "It's time for me to step down and choose the next CEO. I've decided to choose one of you."
>
> The young executives were shocked, but the boss continued. "I'm going to give each one of you a seed today— one very special seed. I want you to plant the seed, water it, and come back here one year from today with what

you've grown from the seed I've just given you. I will then judge the plants that you bring, and the one I choose will be the next CEO."

A man named Jim was there that day; and he, like the others, received a seed. He went home and excitedly told his wife the story. She helped him get a pot, soil, and compost; and he planted the seed. Everyday, he watered it and watched to see if it had grown. After about three weeks, some of the other executives began to talk about their seeds and the plants that were beginning to sprout.

Jim kept checking his seed, but nothing ever grew.

Three weeks, four weeks, then five weeks went by, but still nothing grew. By now, others were talking about their plants, but Jim still didn't have anything, and he felt like a failure.

Six months went by—still there was nothing in Jim's pot. He just knew he'd killed his seed. Everyone else had trees and tall plants, but he had nothing. Jim didn't say anything to his colleagues, however. He just kept watering and fertilizing the soil. He so wanted the seed to grow.

A year finally had passed, and all the young executives of the company took their plants to the CEO for inspection.

Jim told his wife that he wasn't going to take an empty pot, but she asked him to be honest about what happened. Jim felt sick to his stomach. It was going to be the most embarrassing moment of his life, but he knew his wife was right. He took his empty pot to the boardroom.

When Jim arrived, he was amazed by the variety of plants grown by the other executives. They were beautiful, in all shapes and sizes. Jim put his empty pot on the floor, and many of his colleagues laughed, although a few felt sorry for him.

When the CEO arrived, he surveyed the room and greeted his young executives, while Jim just tried to hide in the back.

"My, what great plants, trees, and flowers you've grown," said the CEO. "Today one of you will be appointed the next CEO!"

All of a sudden, the boss spotted Jim at the back of the room with his empty pot. He ordered the financial director to bring Jim to the front.

Jim was terrified. He thought, *The CEO knows I'm a failure! Maybe he'll have me fired!*

When Jim got to the front, the boss asked what had happened to his seed, so Jim told him the story.

The CEO then asked everyone to sit down except Jim. He looked at the young man and then announced to the other executives, "Behold your next chief executive officer. His name is Jim!"

Jim couldn't believe it. He couldn't even grow a seed.

"How could he be the one?" the others asked.

Then the CEO said, "One year ago today, I gave everyone in this room a seed. I told you to take the seed, plant it, water it, and bring it back to me today. But I gave you all boiled seeds—they were dead. It wasn't possible for them to grow. All of you, except Jim, have brought me trees and plants and flowers. When you found that the seeds wouldn't grow, you substituted new ones. Jim was the only person with the courage and honesty to bring me a pot with my seed in it. Therefore, he's the one who will be the new CEO "

If you plant honesty, you'll reap trust.

If you plant goodness, you'll reap friends.

If you plant humility, you'll reap greatness.

If you plant perseverance, you'll reap contentment.

If you plant consideration, you'll reap perspective.

If you plant hard work, you'll reap success.

If you plant forgiveness, you'll reap reconciliation.

So, be careful what you plant now—it will determine what you'll reap later.

Reflection

How much integrity do you have? Do you always keep your word? If you believe there are times it's okay not to keep your word, have you stopped to think about the demarcation between what's acceptable to you and what isn't? Taking the time to consider this distinction will help you define who you wish to be. Perhaps it will also provide you with a personal goal to strive for.

CHAPTER 5

WHO AM I?

"I love you not only for what you are but
for what I am when I am with you."

— ROY CROFT

When Buddha admonished all people to incorporate the recognition "I am the miracle" into their self-talk, he was referring not to himself but to each and every one of us—then and now.

For me, life is a miracle. In fact, I believe that the world would be a dull place indeed if it was just some accidental event in a universe of random chaos, a matter of some fluke or mutation in an evolutionary scheme of nothing back to nothingness. There are, however, many who believe just this, and they don't find the world to be dull at all. I know this to be a fact, for I've shared many hours of conversation with some devout practitioners of scientism (the belief that science is the absolute and only justifiable access to the truth, and as with other religious patterns, there are several degrees of belief within their ranks). These people are atheist about everything except their brand of scientism. Still, life is a miracle for me, and living is a miraculous adventure.

In the 17th century, Blaise Pascal wrote in his *Pensées:*

> When I consider the short duration of my life, swallowed up in the eternity that lies before and after it, when I consider the little space I fill and see, engulfed in the infinite immensity of spaces of which I am ignorant, and which know me not, I rest frightened, and astonished, for there is no reason why I should be here rather than there. Why now rather than then? Who has put me here? By whose order and direction have this place and time been ascribed to me?

When I think of who I am, what comes first to my mind is what I am not. I don't think of myself as a thing, a noun. I don't think of myself as Eldon Taylor: author, husband, father, and horse enthusiast; nor do I think of myself in terms of physical attributes such as six feet tall with dark hair (what's left of it) and so forth. Rather, I'm on record as thinking of myself more in terms of a verb.

I Am an Experience

I'm an experience, experiencing all that comes to me. Once I recognized this subtle but important distinction, it became easier for me to understand the value behind every event. Indeed, I'm only what I do and encounter, for the rest will be left in the ashes of cremation someday. In other words, when time runs out in this life, I won't take anything with me but my experiences—and perhaps you're one of them, so you may take me with you as well.

The question "Who am I?" is answered with "I am an experience." "Why am I?" and "What does that mean?" are different subjects. What's behind the fact that I exist at all is yet another issue. Religion and spirituality seek to answer the latter queries and sometimes confuse the first one by coming up with all kinds of schemes that promise to keep us around in some physical form for eternity. Naturally, we anthropomorphize our gods because it only makes sense that if we remain physical in appearance, then our deities should share this same image. I believe that this is a disservice to God and ourselves, but with this kind of thinking, I can easily understand why there are so many people poking holes in religion and teaching scientism today.

What is it that underpins my being an experience? I am the consciousness that I'm experiencing; and by using my mind in special ways, I can remember the event, flavor it, evaluate it, and even erase it from conscious recollection if I choose. It's consciousness that savors certain events and discriminates rather harshly against others. Through this medium, I'm aware of myself, my beliefs, my ideas, and my ambitions.

C. G. Jung theorized about a collective unconscious. According to him and many mystics before and since, there exists a universal awareness that holds all ideas, experiences, and more. Indeed, it was Jung who insisted this was a necessary mechanism to explain the consistency of archetypes, the kinds of images that he believed elicited the same response, regardless of the culture (for example, the hero is always thought to be the rescuer or champion, and the maiden is thought to be pure and desirable).

The Bible states that man was made in God's image. Does that mean that my consciousness, my experience, is also a part of the Divine? Is who I am an aspect or subset of who God is? That is, is my consciousness, my experience, a part of God? Is the "Grand Organizing Designer" made of consciousness as well?

The universe is intelligent, and this intelligence manifests everywhere. The acorn always becomes an oak. The body heals itself without our guidance. The universe reveals itself elegantly through mathematics. We know this through our own intelligent observations; our special consciousness makes this possible. Perhaps this is the way that we most resemble our Grand Organizing

Designer. In my view, this makes much more sense than thinking about a man or a throne behind the pearly gates of heaven.

That said, understanding that which is beyond our comprehension is, by definition, technically impossible. The ineffable experience is simply linguistically incapable of being communicated—and in my opinion, so is God. Many standard religious ideas are logically false—they must be. Others are tautologies. In the same way that many of the ideas about the Divine are dependent upon notions that can't be logically instantiated or metaphysically substantiated, so also is the answer to our query "Who am I?"

Why does it matter? What I believe about who I am goes to the foundation of what life means. If I'm a noun, a thing, then the way I behave is based more on reacting to the physical world than on interacting with the environment. In the first case, the noun, I'm like a pool ball being pushed around the table or into a hole by other forces, such as a cue ball or other balls. If I remain focused on my local physical condition, then I probably begin to wonder why the pool player is having at me, especially the way life sometimes seems to come. Using this metaphor, I might wonder, *Is this intended, or was it a bad shot, an untimely bounce against the table rails?* In other words, I'll typically evaluate life as acting upon me. I may even train myself to view the world only this way. As a result, when I'm cut off in five o'clock traffic, the action is done to me. It's never just traffic behaving while I experience it—rather, it's always traffic doing something to me.

As an experience, I interact with life. I feel and undergo things differently, for I'm not separate from the total event—I'm a part of it. I'm not an object being acted upon or acting upon others. Instead, I'm participating in an event—a marvelous one full of wonder and awe. In this way, I can frolic even through painful times, for there's something for me to know in everything that happens. I can be intimate with the feelings that the incident itself engenders, and not my reactions to the balls that collide with me.

I believe that life is an experience, and we're here in part to "taste the chocolate." I've often used this metaphor in interviews, and it's worth repeating. I can imagine a time when, before this life, my consciousness participated in another level of being. There I knew many things—at least mentally.

For example, I probably knew about pole-vaulting before coming here. So play with me a moment, and let's draw out an analogy. Imagine that I use a computer to model this sport. I know the speed of a perfect approach, the angle at which the pole first touches the ground, the arm strength required, the point at which the elbows straighten, and so on. Assume that I model it perfectly, and there on the screen is the image of a perfect pole vault—does that make me a pole-vaulter? I think not.

I view this world analogously to the sports scenario. We can know many things, but doing them is different from knowing. I believe that we're here for the doing—to perfect the knowing. We're experiences performing and thereby exercising our learning. We may also be many other things, but if we bring total focus to the events we're a part of, I believe we'll also experience God in them.

Each new day, I offer up this challenge: *Reveal yourself to me through my experiences this day.* How else could I ever come to know God—or, for that matter, myself?

Reflection

What do you think about this? Do you think of yourself as a noun or a verb? What would happen if you started to collect experiences, to think of all of life as simply an opportunity to experience some more? Would it improve the quality of your days? Is the idea worth trying?

CHAPTER 6

LIFE AND PAIN

"All that we are is the result of what we have thought.
If a man speaks or acts with an evil thought, pain follows him.
. . . If a man speaks or acts with a pure thought, happiness
follows him, like a shadow that never leaves him."

— BUDDHA

John Lennon said that we use ideas of the Divine to measure our pain. Is God that type of concept to you?

Why does life have pain? What is it, after all? Obviously, it's not all alike. There's physical discomfort that comes in different degrees, and there's emotional anguish with its own varying thermostat of intensity. Is pain necessary? Do terrible things have to happen? How can a parent who loses a child to some reckless drunk driver possibly find solace in the notion that suffering is a requisite part of life? I mean, if there is a Creator, couldn't the world have been made without all of that?

There's a story that begs us to ask this serious question: *Is pain useful or necessary for great gain? If so, what is that gain?* I'm not sure if this is a true story, but it's very well known. Before I share it, however, allow me to introduce a point of view that may be helpful.

The Praying Hands

In the Bible, Matthew 6:22 states: "The light of the body is the eye: if therefore thine eye be single, thy whole body shall be full of light." What does it mean to have a single vision? Newer translations have changed this text somewhat, and biblical scholars interpret the phrase as being nothing more than a metaphor, something along the lines of: "pull yourself up by your bootstraps." As a metaphor, which I believe it is, the idea is to remain focused like a meditator on the light of being, yours and others, as I suggested in the last chapter. This also brings to mind the idea of *namaste*—or "I see the God within you."

My wife made the point that to her, this concept relates to seeing further ahead than you might when in pain. For example, when driving instructors teach you how to avoid skids and slides on ice and slippery roads, they tell you to look out in front of you—not where you are but where you're going—and aim to control the vehicle at that point. Seeing the long range provides the ability to end a skid, and perhaps it resets the moment in a way that makes more sense of it all.

With that in mind, here's the story:

In a small village near Nuremberg some six centuries ago, there lived 2 brothers and their 16 siblings. They were the sons of the Elder Albrecht Dürer, an immigrant goldsmith. The boys both wanted to be artists, but they knew that their father couldn't afford to send either of them to the art academy in Nuremberg. So after numerous discussions, the two boys came up with this idea. They agreed to toss a coin with the understanding that the loser would get a job in the nearby mines and use this money to support the winner at the art academy. Then, when the winner of the coin toss had finished his studies, which was expected to take four years, he'd then support his brother, either with sales of his artwork or, if necessary, by also getting a job in the mines.

Albrecht Dürer was the brother who won the toss, and soon he was studying art in Nuremberg. Albert Dürer, who lost, obtained a job in the mines; and for the next four years, worked to finance his brother's schooling. Albrecht quickly gained a great reputation; and by the time he graduated, his etchings, woodcuts, and oils were bringing him considerable earnings.

When Albrecht returned home, his family held a celebratory dinner in his honor. At the end of the meal, the artist rose to his feet and proposed a toast to his brother, without whose help he would have been unable to achieve his ambitions. At the end of his speech, Albrecht turned to his brother and said, "Albert, my beloved brother, it is now your turn to go and study art, and it is my turn to support you."

Rather than expressing his pleasure, however, Albert simply sat there with tears falling down his face. Eventually, he arose and told his family that he couldn't pursue a career in art because the four years in the mines had ruined his hands. All the bones in his fingers had been broken at least once, and the arthritis he now suffered from made it difficult even to hold his glass in order to toast his brother, let alone the tools necessary to create fine art. It was simply too late for Albert to pursue his dreams.

Albrecht Dürer went on to become the greatest northern Renaissance artist, producing altarpieces, other religious works, engravings, portraits, and woodcuts. One of his most famous pieces, *The Praying Hands,* is said to be a drawing of Albert's hands.[1]

What does this story mean to you? Was the brother correct to sacrifice so much? In the alternative, was Albrecht then indebted to his brother, needing to somehow repay him in ways not originally agreed to? If you were Albert and had made these sacrifices, would you be proud of your brother's achievements, or would you hold other emotions such as bitterness or jealousy? This is a story about siblings. Would it be any different if the sacrifice were made for a child, a parent, or a stranger?

Faith and Strength

For me, there's no simple answer to the question: *Why pain?* There is, however, a potential perspective that redefines suffering as simply life, in which many things have no immediate or easy answer. The philosopher Søren Kierkegaard was convinced that having absolute proof of God leads to abdicating our ability to hold faith. Without that ability, the vitality of life loses its power. So think of it this way: you're eternal, and if you don't do things right, your parents will punish you. Do you behave as a good human being because you choose that course of action, or do you do so out of a supervised obligation?

Kierkegaard's form of existentialism provides at least a philosophical framework for why there's pain in the world. We can have the perspective that God is benevolent, but then the presence of pain forces us to accept him on faith; or we can think that God intends for us to suffer in order to establish our faith. But in either event, Kierkegaard's approach offers a foundation upon which to justify anguish in the world. It also can be used to address the so-called problem of evil, which we'll discuss in the next chapter.

Life and Pain

Karma

Again, for me, pain is a part of life. In many ways, it makes us stronger. Without adversity, we fail to have the opportunity to temper our strength. It's convenient to explain away some of the tragic events that beset us in life with notions of karma, dharma, and the like. But although this may seem easy, it fails to be anything other than a judgment tool—not that karma is invalid or doesn't serve a purpose. Indeed, paraphrasing the words of one of my editors, Gyatri Devi, the intent of karma isn't to judge others for what's happening to them; rather, it's to show that we're all 100 percent responsible for who we are.

Although we have free will and are at liberty to choose our actions, we aren't free from the consequences. Karma (and a law of physics) says that for every effect, there's a cause. For every consequence in life, the same is also true—there is a cause. This is one of the most important times when what you believe matters.

Gyatri explained it this way: you can refuse to pay taxes because the government uses a large proportion of those taxes to fund war and corruption, because you don't have the funds, or because you want to use the money for something else; but the result will be the same. You'll be penalized. There's no escape from the consequences, no matter how noble or ignoble the intent may have been. Those who choose to pay taxes because they feel they have no choice are still making a decision—to avoid being punished. As Henry David Thoreau, who was jailed for tax-related civil disobedience, is said to have replied when asked by Ralph Waldo Emerson why he was in jail, "Waldo, the question is, why are *you* out *there?*"

It may seem convenient to blame someone's past life for the hardships he or she bears in this incarnation, but how does that do anything other than provide some reassurance that you don't need to suffer in the same way? Pain comes when you choose to be pained.

We need only reflect on the natural disasters of the past to find quite large extremes in the range of reactions. Some shed tears over the loss of their homes and possessions; for others, the response is gratitude for having survived. Still another group works to inspire their neighbors by helping with searching, cleaning up, and starting the rebuilding process, in spite of having lost everything themselves. Everyone had the freedom to choose their reaction. They didn't necessarily cause the disaster, but they did choose their individual responses.

Gyatri shared her perspective on this with me, both in editing this work and in a separate e-mail. I enjoyed and appreciated her input. She concluded one of her remarks with this thought:

> When I meditate on the subject, I perceive karma as this metaphor: as our aura of tendencies, with a vibrational pattern around it like a jigsaw piece in a puzzle. Sometimes it fits the circumstances, sometimes it has to wait until later in the puzzle to find where it belongs, and sometimes it tries to jam itself into a spot that doesn't work at all. I believe this is how we're drawn to parents and incarnations and how we deal with circumstances. Either our experience has given us the shape we need, and we smoothly flow in the circumstance; or we don't have the right fit yet, and we have to bump around and experience some more, trying on different shapes to see what's the best fit.

The Emperor Moth

Gyatri's perspective reminded me of another story that I love. It suggests both why we might be "bumping" around and why it's sometimes wise to allow others to do their own work.

> A scientist was enamored by the glory and beauty of the emperor moth. Its radiant colors, unique patterns and majestic wingspan inspired him to study the moth. Carefully, he watched a young caterpillar spin a cocoon, and then he took the cocoon to his laboratory where he could observe the process.

Life and Pain

The day finally came that the small, crawling caterpillar had become the elegant emperor moth, and the scientist watched with great excitement as the insect began to gnaw its way out of the cocoon. Its tiny jaws chewed away, trying to exit, but it fell back time and again in what seemed to be exhaustion. The scientist watched as the moth worked and failed.

He began to imagine the moth speaking to him: "Why don't you help me?"

The creature finally pushed its head out and began to work at pulling its body through the small hole it had created. Each attempt seemed to fail. Progress was so slow that it was basically imperceptible.

The scientist looked on, beginning to feel guilty for not coming to the aid of the moth. The day was coming to an end, and the progress had been so minute that the scientist finally couldn't hold back. With the spirit of a rescue worker, he took his tweezers and carefully opened the cocoon. The moth was free—but so badly deformed that it couldn't fly. It died soon thereafter.

Later, our scientist learned that it's this very struggle that shapes the insect's body, forcing fluids out to the majestic wings, giving shape to the giant moth. Without the struggle, without the form resulting from the almost torturous requirement to pull itself through a small opening in the cocoon, there is no emperor moth.

So life has its ups and downs, the sun rises and sets, and there are cycles to everything. There are differences in all things, which is precisely how we know them individually. There's light, dark, up, and down. This world of opposites or duality is the one we live in—and this is life. The uncertainty about it all is what makes our journey so robust. Tomorrow we could all be gone—maybe I've been long gone when you read this. But like Pascal's words in the last chapter, the order and direction that have me in this place at this time experiencing what I am now constitutes life—mine and yours. The long view may well provide us with insight, but generally we must wait for some future date before context makes the pain bearable, forgivable, and potentially understandable.

Pragmatics

The pragmatist in me wants to point out the alternative to a theistic perspective at this juncture. Imagine yourself as an atheist, and your seven- or eight-year-old daughter is abducted, raped, and murdered, as in *The Shack,* a thought-provoking book by William Paul Young. What's your long view about why this happened? What an unimaginable and horrible place to be in!

If I believe in God, and I'm wrong because there's no such thing, then at least I've enjoyed a certain comfort by believing otherwise. If atheists are wrong, however, they only harm themselves. The irony is that if they're right, they still hurt themselves. As the theistic existentialist Kierkegaard might well say, "Judge the philosophy by the life of the philosopher and not just the intellectual works."

Our story of the two brothers and *The Praying Hands* illustrates the good that can come from pain and suffering, but it definitely takes an unselfish long view for the brother with bent and twisted fingers to appreciate that benefit. The story of the moth clearly illustrates why pain may be helpful and even necessary. In the end, it's your perception, which is based on belief, that defines pain.

Reflection

How do you think of your life? Do you rage at the injustices and hurts that have been done to you? Are you still holding on to the pains of yesterday? What would happen if you simply trusted that one day you'll discover the silver lining in those particular clouds? Would this attitude assist in making the day of enlightenment arrive even sooner? I believe so. Why not try it and see?

CHAPTER 7

LOVE AND CRUELTY

*"Every age, every culture, every custom and
tradition has its own character, its own weakness
and its own strength, its beauties and cruelties; it accepts
certain sufferings as matters of course, puts up patiently
with certain evils. Human life is reduced to real suffering,
to hell, only when two ages, two cultures and religions overlap."*

— HERMANN HESSE

What is evil? The American poet, Robinson Jeffers, made this interesting observation: "Cruelty is a part of nature, at least of human nature, but it is the one thing that seems unnatural to us." Why is this the case—or is it? Is cruelty evil?

Defining evil may not be quite as easy as it seems if I think of it in the broader sense of its profound effect on our interpretation of the meaning of life. Consulting Webster's dictionary yields this:

1. a : morally reprehensible : sinful, wicked <an evil impulse> b : arising from actual or imputed bad character or conduct <a person of evil reputation>

2. a : archaic : inferior b : causing discomfort or repulsion : offensive <an evil odor> c : disagreeable <woke late and in an evil temper>

3. a : causing harm : pernicious <the evil institution of slavery> b : marked by misfortune : unlucky.[1]

What underlies the conventional definition is the interpretation that intention has a bearing on evil. In other words, unless it's a matter of luck, Webster steers us toward reading in the notion of *mens rea,* or mental intent. Is there a mental state behind a flood, a hurricane, a volcano, or a tsunami—or is it wrong to think of natural catastrophes as evil?

When we hear that a cave-in has taken the lives of a dozen miners, do we think of evil? What about when a tsunami kills thousands or a family loses their home to fire?

Many people would say there's evil in the world, so obviously there's no God—or if there is, he's *not* the one you profess. Perhaps your God is a trickster, and you're just being played with like a cat playing with a mouse—or maybe your creator is dead!

Is it evil when a couple mortgages their home to pay for medical bills, only for one of them to die of the very disease they were treating and then to have their home taken by the bank because everything went to health-care expenses? Must evil always be accompanied by bad luck or intent?

How do we understand this concept? Is evil, as Saint Augustine argued, only that which is a deprivation of good? In other words, an act is evil if it's missing good; but if that's so, what about natural disasters? Is there supposed to be something positive in the volcano that wipes out an entire city? If there's anything like a good God who witnesses all and can act in an intercessory manner, then why is there such suffering by so many innocents in the world? Or are we simply circling around pain, as we discussed in the last chapter?

Intent

First, let me state my bias. Evil must be accompanied by malicious intent—everything else is just life. The hows and whys behind much of life are simply not something we're able to apprehend. I think of it this way: imagine that there's truth in the idea that in the beginning there was only God. The Divine somehow contemplated itself and divided itself into all we know. This is substantially the creation story from most religions and remarkably similar to theoretical physicist Stephen Hawking's account of the big bang, in which singularity somehow divides itself and creates all things. Pursue this further, and the next standard that can be applied has to do with the interpretation of this creation story. If there was only God, then he exists in all of us—the kingdom of heaven is within.

All right, use a little extra imagination, and like the philosophy espoused in process theology, think of yourself as a cell in the body of God. For that matter, to make it more real, think of yourself as one of the approximately 100 trillion cells in your body. Now let's assume that you are the brightest of cells, and you truly wish to understand the concept of the Whole—the God you inhabit and that inhabits you—for after all, you have the perfect cloning capacity to replicate the entire being in just this one cell. So you set out on an adventure. You travel from one end of the body to the other, investigating all of the various parts, mechanics, electrochemical processes and so forth.

You now know this entity perfectly—from the inside. How does this in any way qualify you to apprehend what the body is doing in the outside world? Knowing all of the parts internally isn't the same as understanding the whole externally, nor is it the same as understanding the hows and whys behind the being's thinking or the intelligence of it all as discussed in Chapter 5.

Next, think of yourself as a neurologist, examining neurons. You know that they're basically analog in their intake and digital in their output. You know what their action potential is, and you've witnessed their continuous background. You've seen groups of neurons become excited and increase their rate of firing. Like the earlier pole-vaulting scenario, you know all of the detail regarding how neurons work, even though in reality, this is something we still don't really completely understand. Nevertheless, even if you did, would this tell you what the brain was thinking? The answer is a certain "No!"

There are matters that simply cannot be satisfactorily answered, and they never have been. That, too, is just life.

Returning to our subject, the evil that occurs as a result of intention is created by humans. We can't say that it's evil for a cat to follow its instincts and torture a mouse. The word torture doesn't even apply, for that intent isn't involved when we call something instinct. The behavior of the so-called lower animal kingdom is void of this kind of determination, so the question we're left with is *Why are some humans evil?*

The fact is that this malevolent force is of human making. Whether it's a social group that infects the good with such notions as "It's okay to get even," which unfortunately we see too much of today, or it's a special case of a disturbed individual, evil is a human being acting with a deprivation of good.

It's my belief that this form of socialization is a perversion of the virtue that human beings know should be their nature. A worthy act is a loving one. The Golden Rule may well fit here, for a loving act is also a genuine case of treating someone else as we would want to be treated. Research shows that small children recognize when something immoral is done to other children, such as taking their toys for no reason or slapping them without provocation.[2] We inherently seem to understand the principle of precedent and reciprocity, even if it's selfish in some ways.

Epicurus put the problem this way:

Either God wants to abolish evil and cannot; or he can but does not want to. If he is willing but not able, he is impotent. If he is able but not willing, he is malevolent. If he is both willing and able, then whence comes evil? If he is neither willing nor able, then why call him God?

Accordingly, God would have to either abolish the human race or do away with free will. I tend to side with C. S. Lewis on this one, as he outlines his views in *Mere Christianity:*

> My argument against God was that the universe seemed so cruel and unjust. But how had I got this idea of just and unjust? A man does not call a line crooked unless he has some idea of a straight line. What was I comparing this universe with when I called it unjust? If the whole show was bad and senseless from A to Z, so to speak, why did I, who was supposed to be part of the show, find myself in such violent reaction against it? A man feels wet when he falls into water, because man is not a water animal: fish would not feel wet. Of course I could have given up my idea of justice by saying it was nothing but a private idea of my own. But if I did that, then my argument against God collapsed too—for the argument depended on saying that the world was really unjust, not simply that it did not happen to please my fancies. Thus in the very act of trying to prove that God did not exist—in other words, that the whole of reality was senseless—I found I was forced to assume that one part of reality—namely my idea of justice—was full of sense. Consequently atheism turns out to be too simple. If the whole universe has no meaning, we should never have found out that it has no meaning: just as, if there were no light in the universe and therefore no creatures with eyes, we should never know it was dark. Dark would be a word without meaning.[3]

Absence of Good

Just or unjust, cruel or loving, good or evil, moral or immoral —these pairs of opposites are interpretations by human beings and intended as remedies to and by the actions of human beings. The next time you think of the problem of evil, think of the intent, the human involvement, and the absence of good that could be present.

I believe that with this view, we can manage to improve our world, if we will but take responsibility to do something that promotes the good. It's the good intent, the belief that the human condition can exist in peace and know prosperity and abundance in the process, that will make this possible.

No amount of nay-saying will ever get us closer to justice or closer to our own potential. Karma and dharma aren't supposed to be excuses for wickedness in this world, but many attempt to use them in this way. Thus evil finds an acceptable way into our thinking and expectations and therefore our realities. There's never a long-term solution when blame is the lever and excuses are the fulcrum. No amount of rationalization or accusation, whether founded in fact or fiction, will ever lead us to extinguishing evil. We vanquish it by recognizing that its source rests in the human dimension and therefore so does its cure.

The Mayonnaise Jar

I was once sent an e-mail that contained a wonderful story designed to encourage and uplift, even in times of woe when things seem too much to handle. If you've ever experienced a setback, a time you'd like to forget, or even what we might call evil in your life, then remember the story of the mayonnaise jar.

When things in your life seem almost too much to handle, when 24 hours in a day is not enough, remember the mayonnaise jar and two cups of coffee.

A professor stood before his philosophy class with some items on the lectern in front of him. When the class began, he wordlessly picked up a very large and empty mayonnaise jar and proceeded to fill it with golf balls.

He then asked the students if the jar was full. They agreed that it was.

The professor next picked up a box of pebbles and poured them into the jar. He shook the jar lightly. The pebbles rolled into the open areas between the golf balls.

He asked the students again if the jar was full. They agreed it was.

The professor then picked up a box of sand and poured it into the jar. Of course, the sand filled up everything else. He asked once more if the jar was full.

The students responded with a unanimous "Yes."

The professor brought two cups of coffee from under the table and poured the entire contents into the jar, effectively filling the empty space between the sand.

The students laughed.

"Now," said the professor, as the laughter subsided, "I want you to recognize that this jar represents your life. The golf balls are the important things: God, family, and children. If everything else were lost and only they remained, your life would still be full.

"The pebbles are the other things that matter, such as your job, house, and car. The sand is everything else—the small stuff.

"If you put the sand into the jar first," he continued, "There's no room for the pebbles or the golf balls.

"The same goes for life. If you spend all your time and energy on the small stuff, you'll never have room for the things that are important to you. So . . . pay attention to the things that are critical to your happiness. Play with your children. Take time to get medical checkups. Take your partner out to dinner. Play another 18 holes of golf.

"There will always be time to clean the house and fix the garbage-disposal unit. Take care of the golf balls first— the things that really matter. Set your priorities. The rest is just sand."

One of the students raised her hand and asked what the coffee represented.

The professor smiled. "I'm glad you asked. It just goes to show you that no matter how full your life may seem, there's always room for a couple of cups of coffee with a friend."

The email ended with this note: "Please share this with someone you care about." I just did!

Reflection

Good is measured in how we treat others. What is it that you believe? Are you one of those people who doesn't believe that evil even exists, who contends that it's just an illusion, something we constructed in our minds? Can you think of some malevolence that's not of human making? Do you believe that for something to be evil, it must be accompanied by malicious intent? Do you consider that it's the belief in evil that creates it, and therefore all you need do is love it away? If you and all your friends got together and sent love to those in Afghanistan who believe that a woman should be beaten for speaking too loudly, what do you think the effect would be? Even if you think it would have a positive effect, would this be enough to save all those women? What's the practical application of your belief? Is there a better way?

CHAPTER 8

THE GODS OF SCIENCE

"The idea of a universal Mind or Logos would be, I think, a fairly plausible inference from the present state of scientific theory."
— ARTHUR EDDINGTON

There's a myth about the tension between science and religion. Unfortunately, many scientists have been duped by this fable, so allow me to begin by setting the record straight. The truth is that science and religion were handmaidens to each other throughout most of history. The great scientists of the past believed they were discovering insights into God's handiwork—not exceptions.

The myth, often referred to as the "Conflict" or "Warfare" thesis, asserts that science and religion have been at odds throughout history. Indeed, in this version of events, this antagonism has held science back in the past.

Politics and Science

Where did this myth have its genesis? During the late 19th century, two men with similar political motives created the story of warfare between religion and science. John William Draper (1811–1882) was a chemist and the first president of the American Chemical Society. He was also a physician and the son of an English Methodist minister. His 1874 book was titled *History of the Conflict Between Religion and Science*. The book flatly misstated many facts, twisting the evidence to fit Draper's agenda. No decent scholar today takes the work seriously. Indeed, it's an example of "bad history!"[1] According to Professor Lawrence M. Principe of Johns Hopkins University, "The text is actually one long, vitriolic, anti-Catholic diatribe."[2]

There are reasons for Draper's strong disapproval of Catholicism, including the fact that he was a Protestant, and he chose to align Protestantism with science, using the First Vatican Council's declaration against rationalism as his wedge against the church. Principe notes: "Although Draper's work is easy to dismiss as cranky and ahistorical, his theme and many of his anecdotes have entered the common consciousness, where they have remained hard to remove."[3]

The second man to formalize the fictional battle was Andrew Dickson White. In his would-be authoritative text, *A History of the Warfare of Science with Theology in Christendom,* White masquerades as a historian when in truth his work is probably an outstanding example of poor scholarship. It has been said that this work belongs in a museum dedicated to the "how not to do" world of academics.[4]

So who was this man, and why did he write this two-volume work? White was the first president of Cornell University, which was the first university in this country without religious affiliation.

Indeed, most believe that he was prompted to write because of the criticism leveled at him for establishing the school in this way.[5]

His book is full of fallacious assertions and, quite frankly, absolutely bogus sources. He advanced many false arguments, including the notion that the world was believed to be flat before Christopher Columbus's voyage.[6] As incorrect as this assertion is, it's still taught today, and just as with White's erroneous claims about the battles between religion and science, most people still believe this nonsense.

Just think for a moment: the Greek astronomer Eratosthenes, around 245 B.C., calculated the circumference of the Earth within 1 percent of its actual size as we know it today. This knowledge wasn't lost, but like the falsehood regarding the so-called war between religion and science, the myth lives on in the minds of many.

Again, I return to Principe's words: "Besides poor scholarship, these books rely on a central and fallacious assumption: that scientists and theologians formed two separate camps throughout history and that theologians imposed their will on scientists. . . . The pre-modern thinkers retroactively called scientists themselves believed that theology and religious texts were relevant to their work and vice versa."[7]

If there never was a war between science and religion before the distinction falsely drawn by Draper and White, why then does this falsehood continue to be argued today? It's all in the definitions—and once again, that leads us to an inspection of motive. What's the agenda of those who like to draw upon this myth as a basis for their religious intolerance, skepticism, and outright efforts at conversions to atheism?

Materialistic and Reductionistic

If I choose to become a convert to this atheistic view of the world, then I might accept, as artificial-intelligence theorist Eliezer Yudkowsky puts it in *Less Wrong:*

Part of the rationalist ethos is binding yourself emotionally to an absolutely lawful reductionistic universe—a universe containing no ontologically basic mental things such as souls or magic—and pouring all your hope and all your care into that merely real universe and its possibilities, without disappointment.[8]

Fortunately, there are still those who have not been seduced by this movement.

What exactly is the materialistic reductionistic perspective? Materialism is the belief that everything that exists does so in the material (physical) world. There are no spirits, souls, life beyond death, or psychic or higher realities of any kind.

The reductionistic perspective adds some caveats, holding that everything is reducible to some smaller unit, a new twist on the old atomist philosophy. The mental aspect of life, according to this point of view, is nothing more than sense impression combinations. As such, this perspective offers no metaphysical element to life whatsoever.

Why is this philosophy so able to capture the interest of young people everywhere? Indeed, according to the latest data, 80 percent of the people of Sweden don't believe in God, nor do 39 percent of the people in the United Kingdom, more than 60 percent of all the scientists in the United States, and the list goes on—and is growing.[9]

The attractiveness of the materialist reductionistic philosophy appears to arise as a result of old definitions. I say this because that's what the champions of atheism attack. As I suggested earlier, when the religious world gives their God human attributes—a male sitting on some throne in heaven, surrounded by angels and harps, an all-good (omnibenevolent), all-knowing (omniscient), all-powerful (omnipotent) being, who created everything from nothing in six days (just a few thousand years ago)—it's no wonder that the intelligentsia back away.

Think of it this way: imagine a round square. Can an all-powerful God build a rock so large that he can't lift it? Could God have created Adam with a perfect will instead of the deficient character that led to his sin? If he could have, then whose defect caused the fall from grace? There are so many self-contradictory aspects to these definitions that it's surprising they've lasted as long as they have. Additionally, what kind of heaven is it where we all sit around listening to harp music—something that, as Mark Twain said, we'd hate to do in this life.

More modern attempts to redefine God have removed some of the anthropomorphic characteristics and made the deity androgynous. When you begin to redefine the spiritual and then ask people about their beliefs, you get a different picture. For example, in the United Kingdom, where only 38 percent believe in God, another 40 percent believe in life force or spirit; in France, where only 34 percent believe in God, you can add another 27 percent by including spirit; and in the United States, when you look only at those who don't believe either in God or spirit or life force, the number diminishes to 6 percent.

However, author and secularist Sam Harris reminds us:

> Although it is possible to be a scientist and still believe in God—as some scientists seem to manage it—there is no question that an engagement with scientific thinking tends to erode, rather than support, religious faith. Taking the U.S. population as an example: Most polls show that about 90% of the general public believes in a personal God; yet 93% of the members of the National Academy of Sciences do not. This suggests that there are few modes of thinking less congenial to religious faith than science is.[10]

Taking this notion one step further, in his book *The God Delusion,* Richard Dawkins quotes an article in *Mensa Magazine* (Mensa is the society for people with high IQs): "Of 43 studies carried out since 1927 on the relationship between religious belief and one's intelligence and/or educational level, all but four found an inverse connection."[11]

The Necessary God

The truth is, however, that many scientists today find God is almost a necessary implicit aspect of how and why the world reveals itself to us as it does. In fact, and perhaps contrary to popular belief and therefore definitely worthy of repeating, I'll share just a couple of comments by Nobel laureates.

When asked the question, "Many prominent scientists—including Charles Darwin, Albert Einstein, and Max Planck—have considered the concept of God very seriously. What are your thoughts on the concept of God and on the existence of God?" Christian Anfinsen, Nobel Prize winner in chemistry, replied:

> I think only an idiot can be an atheist. We must admit that there exists an incomprehensible power or force with limitless foresight and knowledge that started the whole universe going in the first place.[12]

George Wald, Nobel Prize winner in medicine and physiology, said:

> When it comes to the origin of life there are only two possibilities: creation or spontaneous generation. There is no third way. Spontaneous generation was disproved one hundred years ago, but that leads us to only one other conclusion, that of supernatural creation. We cannot accept that on philosophical grounds; therefore, we choose to believe the impossible: that life arose spontaneously by chance!

There are, of course, many others, and a quick online search will yield a book's worth. But just as important as the statements from modern minds are those of the past. In that sense, René Descartes, founder of analytical geometry and modern dualistic philosophy, put the matter this way:

> I have always been of the opinion that the two questions respecting God and the Soul were the chief of those that ought to be determined by help of Philosophy rather than of Theology; for although to us, the faithful, it be sufficient to hold as matters

of faith, that the human soul does not perish with the body, and that God exists, it yet assuredly seems impossible ever to persuade infidels of the reality of any religion, or almost even any moral virtue, unless, first of all, those two things be proved to them by natural reason. And since in this life there are frequently greater rewards held out to vice than to virtue, few would prefer the right to the useful, if they were restrained neither by the fear of God nor the expectation of another life.[13]

There are pragmatic reasons for believing in life after death. One such reason might be in explaining to a small child (or to yourself, for that matter) where a deceased loved one has gone. There are also intuitive reasons. That is, we're hardwired for religious perception. As I've pointed out in my earlier books, stimulate certain areas of the brain, and it seems possible to provoke a deep religious experience. Now, we might argue that this is only some vestige of evolution, a throwback to something we needed at some time for survival purposes, and I accept that idea, despite its improbability. I would go further though, at this juncture—indeed, as I did in my book *Mind Programming*—and point out that with this natural state of existence, 1) it's no wonder that religion has been with us throughout history; and 2) it would appear that given this inherited biological fact, to become an atheist we must either be trained or be so deeply disappointed by God that we throw him overboard.

White Crows

There's another issue I want to focus on here, however. I've stated up until now two reasons for believing in life after death—the pragmatic and the natural. There's a third, and this one convinced me.

Many things that happen in the world defy explanation. William James called them the white crows. This refers to the axiom that all crows are black, which means that we need to discover only one white crow in order to disprove this truth. Well, my life has delivered several white crows—miracles, events that defy explanation.[14] Not only have these events happened to me, but in dialogues, lectures, and interviews, I've repeatedly heard similar stories from others. I've often challenged people attending my lectures to think back to something that happened to them that defied explanation, and everyone has been able to do that. Then I ask them why they tucked the memory of this experience away instead of fully integrating it into their understanding of who they are. I suggest that you do the same right now. You might recall a little thing, such as knowing who was on the phone before you answered it, or it could be some life-changing event, such as the story a caller told me during a radio show:

> A small child ran to a home overlooking a cliff and pounded on the door in the middle of the night. When the owner opened the door, the child called for help and led the person to the cliff's edge, where the automobile he'd been riding in with his mother, father, and siblings could be seen. It was crushed and broken apart, and his family members were all dead. The car had been traveling too fast to negotiate a hard turn during a heavy rainstorm and had sailed off the cliff. When law enforcement officers asked the child how he got out of the vehicle, he answered, "A giant hand reached into the car, lifted me out, and set me on the side of the road."

Lady Luck

There's also a wonderful story in *Lady Luck: The Theory of Probability,* by Warren Weaver. The story was first reported in *Life* magazine, and it was shared with me by a listener named Maureen, who heard me speak on a *Coast to Coast AM* radio show.

> All fifteen members of a church choir in Beatrice, Nebraska, due at practice at 7:20, were late on the evening

of March 1, 1950. The minister and his wife and daughter had one reason (his wife delayed to iron the daughter's dress); one girl waited to finish a geometry problem; one couldn't start her car; two lingered to hear the end of an especially exciting radio program; one mother and daughter were late because the mother had to call the daughter twice to wake her from a nap; and so on.

The reasons seemed rather ordinary. But there were ten separate and quite unconnected reasons for the lateness of the fifteen persons. It was rather fortunate that none of the fifteen arrived on time at 7:20, for at 7:25 the church building was destroyed in an explosion.

The members of the choir, *Life* reported, wondered if their delay was "an act of God." Weaver calculates the staggering odds against chance for this uncanny event as about one chance in a million.[15]

Some say that coincidences such as these are almost too purposeful, too orderly, to be a product of random chance, which must strain to accommodate them. But then how do we explain them?

Why does it matter? What you deem to be true matters a lot. If you were to believe that God took personal care of you, watching over and protecting you so long as you lived a certain way, and then something bad happened, you'd either blame yourself or heaven. You might think that you were evil and a lesser person, or these bad things wouldn't happen to you. Alternatively, you might think God placed you here to suffer and thereby prove your worthiness to be saved. Definitions are important, and if yours make you out to be a miserable, pathetic, sinner who deserves to be punished and suffer, then you'll probably experience your self-fulfilling prophecy.

I believe that you were created with unique gifts and abilities. It's up to you to develop and employ these special talents. When you do, you discover that you not only deserve to enjoy this world and all of its wonders but that the miracle you participate in called "life" is just that—one truly incredible white crow, not some ordinary thing taken for granted because it's here every day. Life doesn't suck, and you don't just then die—both it and you are truly miracles!

I'll leave this subject with the words of Antoine de Saint-Exupéry:

> We say nothing essential about the cathedral when we speak of its stones. We say nothing essential about Man when we seek to define him by the qualities of men.[16]

Reflection

I choose to accept the miracle that you are, that I am, that life is! I choose to live that wonder, and I wish for you to realize the miracle that you are! What do you think? Do you believe that science can possibly answer all questions? Do you find conflict between science and spirituality? What about those incidents, either in your own experience or in stories you've heard, that defy all logical explanation? How do you reconcile the two? What would happen if you were to start thinking of your life as a miracle? Would this bring you greater joy? Is it worth a try?

CHAPTER 9

ATTACHED TO UNATTACHMENT

"Better indeed is knowledge than mechanical practice. Better than knowledge is meditation. But better still is surrender of attachment to results, because there follows immediate peace."

— THE BHAGAVAD GITA

I admit to being very attached to some things—including the notion of being unattached. I am invested in the welfare of my family, for example. It's not that I ultimately believe I control their destiny but rather that I would do all that I could for them. Most of us are in this same place.

The Dalai Lama has this to say about attachment:

> As human beings we all want to be happy and free from misery. . . we have learned that the key to happiness is inner peace. The greatest obstacles to inner peace are disturbing emotions such as anger, attachment, fear and suspicion, while love and compassion and a sense of universal responsibility are the sources of peace and happiness.[1]

At the same time, he has actively campaigned for the welfare of Tibet. One might easily say that he's as attached to the welfare of his nation as I am to the welfare of my family.

Saint John of the Cross believed that attachment needed a purification of sorts. Only through becoming unattached were we able to discover meaning. In his view, "If you purify your soul of attachment to and desire for things, you will understand them spiritually. If you deny your appetite for them, you will enjoy their truth, understanding what is certain in them."[2]

There's a lot of conversation nowadays, especially in the pop psychology and New Age venues, about living unattached lives. What does that really mean? How do we truly remain unattached and at the same time hold values, cherish one another, and love the idea of peace? I discussed this idea in my book *Choices and Illusions,* but the bottom line is this: we can achieve this if we change the context some and think of it this way—we're unattached to the outcome.

How does that differ? When I'm attached to someone or something, it actually holds my controls. If I love a person and she leaves me, even decides to despise me, I'll no doubt feel emotional pain. If I didn't, I'd be a sociopath. If I'm attached to the belief that only that individual can make me happy, only she is my true soul mate, what I do is, in effect, surrender my autonomy. That is, I'm no longer in control of my choices or my life—instead, I'll suffer the loss for as long as I hold those beliefs.

On the other hand, if I recognize that my affection for this person is unattached, what I essentially define for myself is unconditional love. In other words, in the first scenario I'm dependent upon someone for my well-being; in the latter, the happiness of the other person is foremost in my mind. It may sound trite, but the truth is that if you really care for someone, and that person needs to be somewhere else, then allowing the loved one that space—even if it means you are abandoned by that person—is what unconditional love is all about.

We raise our children to leave home and become contributing citizens to our society. None of us looks forward to the day that they go; yet like death itself, we know it will most certainly come, one way or another. Letting go of our offspring isn't easy if we depend upon them for some part of our identity—our happiness. On the other hand, when our outlook takes into account the excitement that young people have about being on their own, having their own place and belongings—we can smile and let them go, even cushioning their unspoken fears by letting them know that they're always welcome to come back. For, you see, their home is our home—wherever they are.

Detachment and unconditional love spring from the same fountainhead, yet there are constructs, concepts, ideas, and beliefs that we'll forever remain attached to. For example, I'm invested in the idea of such individual freedoms as life, liberty, and the pursuit of happiness. It's because I am so committed that I do what I can to end the atrocities that occur in the world. When I hear about a 12-year-old girl who's been beaten and disfigured by her husband in Afghanistan, I'm disgusted. I know of no way to say that I'm unattached to the event or its ultimate outcome. When I encounter stories that inspire me, that send goose bumps up my spine, I again can't say that I'm indifferent.

I find the idea of total nonattachment to be unreal. For me, always the pragmatist, the only way I could ever reach that state would be to give up my individuality. It would be akin to arguing for a form of nihilism. The absence of personal identity would be the loss of all those talents and abilities bestowed upon me. It would make no sense to do my best at anything just to become nothing. I'm aware of certain Eastern teachings that espouse this, but again, as Mark Twain might have said, "Why would I spend my life sacrificing in order to obtain something I wouldn't like here on Earth?"

Interdependence

Not many of us actually seek nothing in life. Indeed, we're herd animals, and we need love, recognition, and appreciation just as assuredly as we require food and water. Studies show us that infants left without touch suffer as a consequence; those who are held, touched, stroked, and loved thrive by comparison. Indeed, according to the Touch Research Institute, "Research has shown that babies who receive extra touch have more mature nervous systems. They sleep better at night, grow faster, are less fussy overall, and are generally more social and interactive with their parents."[3a, 3b]

So why would I seek to become nothing? If we're biologically made to share, to be touched, and to be rewarded for this activity, what on earth would prompt me to want to annihilate myself? An escape mechanism? There are indeed many who teach exactly that. Their idea flows from the notion that overcoming ego will result in an immersion of the individual with the total or "One."

There is a marvelous story by an unknown author that touches the nature of our interdependence upon one another:

Just up the road from my home is a field with two horses in it. From a distance, each one looks like any other horse. But if you get a closer look, you'll notice something quite interesting. One of the horses is blind.

His owner has chosen not to have him put down, but has made him a safe and comfortable barn to live in. This alone is pretty amazing. But if you stand nearby and listen, you'll hear the sound of a bell. It's coming from the smaller horse in the field.

Attached to the horse's halter is a small, copper-colored bell. It lets the blind animal know where his companion is so that he can follow. As you stand and watch these two friends, you'll see that the horse with the bell is always checking on the other horse and that the blind horse will listen for the bell and then slowly walk to where the guide horse is, trusting that he won't be led astray. When the horse with the bell returns to the shelter of the barn each evening, he stops occasionally to look back, making sure that the blind friend isn't too far behind to hear him.

The story continues to make a point with respect to God, but it could just as well be made regarding our roles with each other.

Like the owner of these two horses, God doesn't throw us away just because we aren't perfect or because we have problems or challenges. He watches over us and even brings others into our lives to help us when we are in need. Sometimes we're the blind horse, being guided by the little ringing bell of those whom God places in our lives. And at other times we're the guide, helping others to find their way.

A "Personal God"?

At this point, you may wonder if I'm trying to say that there's a personal God. As I thought about this matter, I realized there was no simple answer—no one-liner. Indeed, perhaps that is another book. Still, a brief explanation may be in order.

I see the story of the horses as the God within manifesting by way of the care and concern shared between two animal friends. Each and every one of us has both the divine presence within and the ability to care for and protect our fellow human beings.

I'm on record in many places stating that I believe a fundamental element of the purpose of every human being is service. It's also a biological fact that we're organically rewarded when we go to the aid of others, even if it's only by doing something as simple as writing a check to a charity we care about. The brain releases those feel-good neurochemicals as our built-in bonus.

Whether there's a personal God or not is academic in that sense. I do believe that the divine is beyond the scope of our ability to understand or communicate and that within us is God's presence.

I think of it this way: just as each cell of the body possesses all of the information to reproduce the whole—say, one of your cells producing your clone—each of us lives within the larger body of God. Recall the analogy I presented earlier. As a cell, I might be particularly curious and travel throughout the body, learning all of the parts, the organs, the respiratory system, and so forth, but that would never provide the information that's seen by the whole. Using this framework as a further analogy for our relationship to God, how can we expect to truly comprehend the divine? How can the finite ever comprehend the infinite?

We use the idea of zero every day in mathematics; yet when we divide by zero, the answer is undefined—infinite. We accept that and write computer programs in such a way as to avoid this problem. I accept that my experience informs me of the divine within us all—the love, support, and compassion that are the highest human potential. I allow that my reason will just have to accept and wait to comprehend God. Like the two horses, it is the heavenly within that rings the bell I hear.

Personal Identity

The idea that we're each a drop of water in the ocean can be compelling in some ways. The typical perspective offered in Buddhism postulates that we are drops of water, individualized but for a moment from the greater sea that is the total of all-that-is. I get the idea of immersion, being one with the One. I don't, however, see that as requiring the surrender of my self, and isn't a healthy ego necessary for my identification? I've said before that an ego out of control fits the 12-step-program interpretation of the word: *Edging God Out*. But a healthy ego is who we are.

I know myself in many ways, chiefly as an experience, as I've already discussed. In that sense, I expect that the word *ego* doesn't really apply in its traditional form. For as a verb instead of a noun, I am my experiences—always in motion, dynamic as opposed to static, changing as opposed to immutable, expanding as opposed to contracting, and forever young in every instance as opposed to aging. Still, even in this view, I have a self-concept, and from this spring my lessons, alternatives, choices, likes, and dislikes. This is identity, and it's absolutely attached to the experience, even if part of that is letting go in order to proceed in a new and different way in some other dimension of existence.

I'm totally unaware of any near-death experiences (NDE) in which the survivor tells of being immersed and losing all sense of identification. It's possible, however, to lose our sense of being, to become so involved in the moment that we lose ourselves. That may be what immersion really is. Getting lost in the experience, whether on this plane or another, is experience at its highest.

For me, the analogy of a drop of water in the ocean is fitting when I think of losing myself in the moment. To do that, I must truly choose to engage in everything life brings to me, and that can't be done while unattached. I become the experience by being fully aware of what's happening in each moment. In doing so I can let go of my expectations, for as long as I hold them, I can't be fully present.

Words can be tricky, and ideas can become puzzles, where-as definitions can and do delimit our understanding of all that we care enough to think about. When many of these concepts are distilled, there remain a few constants. One of them is sim-ply this: immersing ourselves in the experience of life gives rise to understanding that we could otherwise never grasp. The little miracles are not only noticed but fully integrated into our journey. The sadness that comes along is recognized for what it is, but this doesn't rob us of hope, for we're not hanging onto some expecta-tion in the moment. Setting about each day with the idea that it's a miracle—that every moment is a wondrous opportunity to glimpse yet another spectacular exchange in the nature of life, a grand time for fully immersing ourselves in the experience—approaches heaven on earth here and now.

The Gift

I believe that every breath is a gift, and what you do with that is the only way you can pay tribute to the Giver. I believe that you were meant to have faith in yourself and that you deserve to know an unlimited cornucopia of abundance in all the good things this life has to offer. When you trust in yourself, you turn the key in the lock that opens the door to manifesting your true potential. You aren't going to take anything with you out of here except your experiences. And notice that it's *you* I believe in—and that calls for the distinctly unique individual that you are—not some generalization. Perhaps I'm attached to an idea of being unattached, at least to an outcome, yet as with everyone else, I'm also committed to being uniquely me. In the end, if I weren't invested in anything, including my experience and ideas, then who would I be?

In the words of novelist Virginia Woolf, "[It] is like a spider's web, attached ever so slightly perhaps, but still attached to life at all four corners. *Often the attachment is scarcely perceptible* [emphasis added]."[4]

Reflection

So what is it that you believe? Do you think that the goal of a spiritual life is to overcome the illusion of separateness, to lose your sense of identity and so to return to the oneness? Or do you believe that this life and your individuality are amazing gifts that should be treasured and experienced to the fullest? Should you be attached to outcomes, or should you focus on doing your best and then detaching? Which beliefs would serve you best?

CHAPTER 10

ENLIGHTENMENT

"Enlightenment is a man's release from his self-incurred tutelage. Tutelage is man's inability to make use of his understanding without direction from another. Self-incurred is this tutelage when its cause lies not in lack of reason but in lack of resolution and courage to use it without direction from another. Sapere aude! 'Have courage to use your own reason'—that is the motto of enlightenment."

— IMMANUEL KANT

Sapere aude is a Latin phrase that means "dare to know." Kant wrote this in "An Answer to the Question: What Is Enlightenment?" in the 18th century. He died in 1804, and his remark has as much bearing on the question of enlightenment today as it did more than 200 years ago.

One of the activities I truly enjoy is hosting my own radio show, *Provocative Enlightenment.* Not long ago, the discussion was all about self-help and personal empowerment. My callers and I spoke at length about how neither can be accomplished without a committed level of self-responsibility. I inserted the idea that enlightenment is also impossible without this quality, which for me means being accountable for everything in my life. As I've said many, many times, we may not be in control of the stimuli that the world brings to us, but we're absolutely in charge of our reactions.

After the show, my son asked me, "So what is enlightenment?"

We spoke for some time about the meaning of life. Then the next morning while I was showering, my thoughts sort of distilled. They came together in a way that I wish to share with you in this chapter.

Enlightenment Is a Process

For me, enlightenment is a process. I think of it as somewhat resembling a light bulb attached to a rheostat. Little by little as the rheostat is turned up, more and more power reaches the bulb, and it begins to shine brighter and brighter.

Using this analogy, the tiniest bit of light is bright at first! In the darkness, even the smallest illumination is appreciated. We move about in total blackness, blind to obstacles and treasures alike. With just a hint of light, we begin to gain some navigation ability and are able to avoid at least the larger impediments. As our radiance grows in strength, it reveals more and more of the path. We begin to find some of the treasures and avoid dangers we might have fallen prey to at an earlier stage in our development.

In time, if we're diligent, the promise is that we'll become enlightened. Such a being is capable of doing the things the Buddha, Jesus, Mahavira (the man who gave Jainism its present-day form), and others have done—heal the sick, feed the hungry, and perhaps one day even walk on water. I know no one who can accomplish that last feat. I do know people who have healed others through prayer, meditation, and other means; and I know many who are committed to healing the planet. To me, that commitment marks an increase in the evolution of the enlightenment process, although just one stage.

I don't see the experience of a miracle as enlightenment. Instead, such encounters wake us up a nudge at a time. They speak to us about possibilities, urging us to delve deeper into our own being and examine our lives with a reverence for the miracle we are. These encounters show us that there's much more to being human than existing as a meat machine that sprang from a random universe through mutation. They coach us to choose once again, and when we do, assuming our choice moves toward the light, our small inner light bulbs grow brighter and brighter.

The Spiritual Experience

I believe that whenever we do our very best at anything we do, we approach a spiritual experience. I've worked with many elite athletes, and they've all expressed how that "sweet moment" of achievement is truly spiritual. Each of us is unique in some way, and expressing the highest ability within our grasp is our way of saying "Thank you" for the gift.

You must "live into" your life—your uniqueness, your experiences, all of who you are—in order to travel the path of enlightenment. Living into who you are includes fully embracing your true self with unconditional love and acceptance. It absolutely requires that you examine yourself, peeling back the layers of falseness, pretense, sound bites, and personas in order to get to the true you. I know this doesn't sound easy, and I guarantee you that it isn't! That said, I also guarantee that there's no more worthy mission if life is to have any meaning beyond I live, I consume, I procreate, and I await my death—or I have died.

Reflection

Enlightenment is a journey that reveals itself to you through your experience. It's therefore by doing your best at everything that you open the door to discovering the meaning of your life. I dare you to be wise and use your own reason. What do *you* think enlightenment is? Is it possible that you're more enlightened than you think you are? How well do you know yourself?

CHAPTER 11

TRYING, LOSING, AND PERSISTING

"Nothing in the world can take the place of persistence.
Talent will not; nothing is more common than unsuccessful
people with talent. Genius will not; unrewarded genius is almost
a proverb. Education will not; the world is full of educated
derelicts. Persistence and determination alone are omnipotent.
The slogan 'Press on' has solved and always will solve
the problems of the human race."

— CALVIN COOLIDGE

In his book *A Better Way to Live*, Og Mandino recounts how he found out how many strikeouts Hank Aaron had while he was earning his home-run title. It turned out that for every home run, Aaron had two strikeouts.

I watched my son strike out during his first baseball game. I could tell that he was anxious to get away from the plate even before he'd taken a swing. He was afraid—he knew inside himself that he would strike out before the first pitch was thrown. From the bleachers, I could only watch and wish I were in the dugout, where I could have said something to him. After the game, I addressed the issue with him, but he was in denial and very sensitive about the matter, so I let it go.

A couple of months later, when the event was ancient history, I took him down to my library and broached the subject again. I asked him to read the three short pages of Mandino's book under "Rule Three." He read the Aaron story, and then we reopened the baseball strikeout issue. This time it was easy to discuss his fear and what failure really means—a new beginning, another chance, and an experience that we learn from.

It's interesting how important a little time can be. Sometimes it takes time before we can discuss something. Sometimes we need to spend more time just listening or being by ourselves or with another person. We have to understand our own expectations and what lies behind them. My son, for example, was afraid he'd strike out—so much so that he made an unconscious plan to do just that. As a result of his fear, his mind actually rehearsed the event. He saw it happening in his mind.

Expectations

Our expectations can heal us, and they can harm us. Many people are afraid of losing, winning, playing, and embracing much that life has to offer. Moving that to a new context—acknowledging our own anticipation while maneuvering it into the zone of practice, trying, learning, and waiting with expectancy of success—is one of the grandest endeavors we can undertake. But to do that, we must at times be both the patient and the healer.

I'm reminded of an old Sufi story about time and pomegranates that may be helpful here:

> Once upon a time, in a land far away, there was a young man who wanted to become a healer. He knew of a legendary healer under whom he wished to train. He therefore set out on a journey to find the man and learn the secrets of his ways.
>
> After a long and trying period, he finally found the healer and without hesitation went up to him. The healer saw that the boy was sincere and decided to take him on as a student.
>
> After weeks of training, the two were sitting on the porch of the healer's modest home when a stranger approached from the distance. He was crumpled over and moved in a peculiar way.
>
> The healer said to his student, "See that man coming up the path? What he needs is pomegranates."
>
> The young man watched as his master listened to the patient tell an agonizing tale of woeful experiences with his affliction, including the struggle he'd gone through just to make the journey to their doorstep.
>
> Finally, the healer put his hand on the patient's shoulder and spoke softly. "Yes, I can see you have suffered. I can see you are ready to leave your illness behind. My friend, I am certain that your disease is due to a shortage of a particular substance available in high concentrations in pomegranates. Eat three a day for the next week, and your health will return."
>
> The patient left and within a couple of weeks returned, standing erect and carrying a basket of food for the healer and the blessings of a deeply grateful self and family.

A short time later, another stranger came down the road. He walked in the same peculiar way and was all bent over.

The student noticed the stranger and excitedly said, "What he needs is pomegranates!"

The healer nodded in agreement without really looking up. The student then pleaded to be allowed to treat the patient. Finally the older man agreed, and the student went out to meet the patient and tell him of his cure.

Approaching the man, the student blurted out, "What you need is pomegranates!"

The stranger stopped. He looked at the student and said, "I came all this way for this nonsense? Pomegranates—rubbish! Some healer you are." And he turned and went away.[1]

This story deals with the expectations of all the parties involved. One aspect of it is that the student didn't understand the necessity of *time* and pomegranates. The afflicted person's assumption that he'd be able to describe his suffering and finally find relief was entirely overlooked by the student. The boy had taken only a mechanical learning from his teacher and assumed that pomegranates alone would cure. For that reason, both the student healer and the patient were disappointed in the end.

When you are both patient and healer, remember to be patient and allow time—time to listen and time to distance and, finally, time to heal.

Quitting

You never lose unless you quit. Vince Lombardi is often quoted as saying, "The difference between winning and losing is quitting." There are thousands of stories about people who failed miserably time after time before finally achieving their goals. They succeeded because they never quit.

Knowing your own limitations is different from quitting, which is a mental state. You may see a ballplayer walking off the field, but long before taking this action, his mind set sail through all the possibilities, reasons, and rationalizations for giving up. He may have even rehearsed the event—to try it on, so to speak—before the actual action. So as I said, it's first a mental action, like my son's strikeout.

There are people I've worked with in the past who persist at quitting. They're not aware that they're giving up, per se, any more than my son was aware that he'd surrendered to striking out before the first pitch was thrown.

Becoming aware of this tendency in ourselves is the only way we can end these self-destructive, self-sabotaging patterns. Persisting should be all about allowing our efforts to become better and better. We persevere at practice—reinforcing our improvement instead of mentally rehearsing our failure expectation. As Marilyn vos Savant is credited with saying, "Being defeated is only a temporary condition; giving up is what makes it permanent."

Winning

I believe that inside every human being is a winner. Each and every one of us possesses a unique ability—a talent, if you will—and chief among all of our abilities is the one called "Doing our very best." I believe that this ability is what makes us champions.

I remember being confused as a young man about such statements as "All men are created equal." It doesn't take an Einstein to see how untrue this statement is—or is it? I tell a story on myself in my book *Choices and Illusions,* in which I made just this inquiry. It seems appropriate here to share what I learned.

Imagine a rocket scientist who, after much work, launches an interstellar voyager. Imagine the pride he feels in the accomplishment. Now imagine a so-called menial laborer. On his hands and knees for endless hours, he scrubs and polishes a floor. He has worked so hard and with so much pride that he has scrubbed his knuckles raw. Now he stands back and beholds his labors. The floor absolutely glistens—every square inch of it. It never looked that good even when it was new. Now . . . which man senses the most pride, the rocket scientist or the floor scrubber?[2]

Even at a young age, I understood that feeling. The fact is that when you do your utmost, you enjoy the same state of specialness, the same ecstatic feeling, the same sense of purpose and pleasure as anyone else, regardless of the act (launching rockets or scrubbing floors).

I believe there are no real losers because in the end, you cannot escape yourself. You—both here and in the hereafter—will learn to persevere, and in time you'll turn the act of trying or the pattern of losing into winning because that's who you ultimately are! You'll acquire the habit of applying your best to all that you do, and as the rocket scientist–floor scrubber story illustrates, that means you'll always come out ahead. You were created a winner, and a winner you were meant to be. Believing in yourself makes winning happen, so the only question is what you're going to do to reinforce a strong, vital faith in yourself—for what you believe always matters!

Always remember the following analogy from Alfred Adler. It's one of my favorites, and it will help you remember to believe in yourself along the way, even when you feel you're drowning.

> What do you first do when you learn to swim? You make mistakes, do you not? And what happens? You make other mistakes, and when you have made all the mistakes you possibly can without drowning—and some of them many times over—what do you find? That you can swim? Well—life is just the same as learning to swim! Do not be afraid of making mistakes, for there is no other way of learning how to live![3]

Reflection

The only way you lose is by quitting. Failure becomes permanent only when you give up. When you visualize quitting, you're rehearsing the event. Can you think of examples from your own life when you were so convinced you'd be unsuccessful that you never even tried? Isn't this often the most basic frustration that people have during a midlife crisis? Do you dare to look again at those dreams you once had and discarded—and to try again, this time with persistence, determination, and tenacity?

CHAPTER 12

GOALS AND AMBITIONS

"Any person who selects a goal in life which can be fully achieved, has already defined his own limitations."

— CAVETT ROBERT

We all set goals, and we all have ambitions, so what makes the difference between the relative successes people enjoy from this process? Cavett Robert, founder of the National Speakers Association, was definitely onto one of the most significant factors in the process of achieving a goal. Think about it this way: If your aim can be fully achieved, then it fails to challenge you sufficiently for you to discover your limitations.

Let's say I set a goal to stop smoking. I quit, so I've succeeded. What's my next project? Do I then set a goal to create an organization, effort, or product to support other smokers in their efforts to kick the habit? Did I give up cigarettes because they're inherently bad for me and for society, or because I was an addict, or for some other reason? There's always a larger perspective, if I but think about it a while.

The smoking example is a simple way to look from a partial view to the bigger picture. If my real goal is to live long, be healthy and fit, and set a good example for my loved ones, then smoking is but one small fraction of that whole. On the other hand, if part of my ambition includes doing my best to make quitting easier for others, to serve and help my fellow human beings, then taking up a cause to end smoking altogether may well represent some portion of my whole goal.

Short-Term Goals

Shortsighted ambitions are those that terminate when some point is achieved. One of my favorite questions is, *How high is up?* Goals should be created from the perspective of the whole and the query, *How much can I do and achieve?* Only in this way do they test who we are instead of defining our limitations.

I remember wanting a special horse facility. I'd successfully created the first horse condominium in the world, franchised the idea, and then sold the system. I next had the idea of a one-stop horse center, a place where you could buy your cowboy boots, breed your mare, put your animal in training, pick up your feed, and so forth. If it had to do with horses or the associated lifestyle, this place would have it: clothing, tack, leather goods, feed, even the animals themselves—all for sale, rent, or lease.

I thought this was a terrific idea, and because I loved spending as much time as I could with horses, I decided to take it on. I found a facility that backed onto a racetrack and bordered a county-owned arena. *A perfect location,* I thought.

I visualized getting all of the money necessary, and when my Small Business Administration loan was approved, I was off to the races, as the saying goes. My goal was to create this facility, and that's what I did. I called it simply "The Horse Store." I even purchased a vacuum truck that could be used to clean out manure for other owners as well as in my own facility. My favorite aspect of the entire operation was the All-Breed Stallion Station, where we stood some outstanding stallions from most registries. So from racing stable and stallion station, to clothing store with feed, to the lot with trailers and portable fencing, this was a one-stop center.

Once built, I realized just how much work it was going to be to run the entire thing and the problems involved in getting help capable of dividing up the many parts and supervising them properly. I'd paid no attention to the economy at large during the dreaming and building of a soon-realized short-term goal—and then things went south. The prime interest rate was suddenly 24 percent and higher. My half-million-dollar loan was costing me more $20,000 each month in interest alone, and the value of recreational anything sagged something fierce!

I was lucky not to end up in bankruptcy over this one, but I learned many things and among them is this: Visualizing the creation, the loan approval, and the goal in general had better include its continued success, or you may find yourself coming up short in the long run. The foresight must be long term!

I'm reminded, however, of the earlier chapter in which I discussed winning, which brings to mind another quotation from the late Cavett Robert that's very fitting:

> If we study the lives of great men and women carefully and unemotionally we find that, invariably, greatness was developed, tested and revealed through the darker periods of their lives. One of the largest tributaries of the *river of greatness* is always the *stream of adversity.*[1]

Long-Term Goals

We all have our streams of adversity, and they do, when we look back, make us who we are. My purpose is to point out the long-range opportunities that exist in all goals and ambitions.

My son Roy intends to become a physicist; when I ask him why, it turns out that it's because he loves physics. My youngest son, William James, wants to be a doctor; when I ask him why, his answer is to help people.

When you define your ambition in terms of your purpose, you can find a much larger horizon than just finishing school with the appropriate degree, as in the case of my two young sons. Doing something because you enjoy it is admirable and certainly what you should do whenever possible. Nonetheless, many things give pleasure, and not all of them have any purpose other than entertainment. If life is to have meaning, it will largely be defined by what you do and how you do it—although that isn't necessarily limited to your vocation. Still, for most people, work will play a significant role in happiness when reflecting back on who you are and what you might have achieved.

The nature of the vocation isn't as important as the attitude that you bring to it. As you've already seen, the floor polisher can achieve the same amount of satisfaction from doing his best as anyone else can. So one element of attitude is this notion of doing your utmost at whatever you might undertake.

The second element of attitude, and just as important, is the attitude you have toward what you do. If, for instance, you're an attorney and you seek to be the best in your field, you may in the process actually compromise some of your principles in order to come out on top, since winning defines the "very best." If, however, you're in the field so that you can help people, then your attitude is much different. It's no longer just about winning regardless of who's right, as with a high-school debate in which you practice both sides of an argument and the entire purpose is simply to come out on top. Rather, it's about serving the people you call clients in the best interest of all concerned. The same principle holds true for everyone: police officer, plumber, or street sweeper.

When you see the bigger picture and incorporate it in your ambitions, goals, and then lifestyle, what you find is a new definition of what you do. Answering the question *How high is up?* when it comes to how much you can contribute to life is both a lofty goal and a worthy ambition. True prosperity is when you breathe your last breath and in your heart of hearts, you believe you did your best, given the circumstances and your level of understanding at the time. I hope this book in some small way makes closing your eyes for the last time a little easier. It's certain that doing your best with the proper attitude will lead you to believe in yourself, and that will facilitate your confidence in dealing with whatever comes your way.

Reflection

Combining your best efforts with the intention to serve can turn any vocation into a genuinely meaningful contribution to yourself and to society. True prosperity comes from knowing that you did your best, and that is the highest of aims.

So what are you striving toward today? How much time have you put into defining these goals? Have you truly analyzed them to discover what your real ambitions are? If you do so, will it cause you to change or modify your intentions at all? And what about the outcome—what do you think your updated goals will give you?

CHAPTER 13

COMPETITION

"The essence of competitiveness is liberated when we make people believe that what they think and do is important— and then get out of their way while they do it."

— JACK WELCH

My father served in World War II under General George Patton, and to my father, Patton was simply the best we had. I remember well being told of the general's arrival in Africa and how he took on the Desert Fox, General Rommel, to defeat the fearsome panzer. My father received a Purple Heart for his service in Africa and was shipped back stateside, where he finished out the war as a drill instructor at Fort Ord. Patton had several sayings, and one that I was raised with, implied every day in the expectation my dad had of his sons, is well expressed in this quotation:

> Battle is the most magnificent competition in which a human being can indulge. It brings out all that is best; it removes all that is base. All men are afraid in battle. The coward is the one who lets his fear overcome his sense of duty. Duty is the essence of manhood.[1]

When I was a boy, this sense of duty and definition of bravery fit very well with the movies and heroes of the day, so of course I bought it, hook, line, and sinker. Is it true today? Was it ever really the case? Is battle anything other than the worst imaginable conduct human beings can undertake? That said, is duty the "essence" and if so, of whom or what?

I've given this issue much thought. It seems that our world works very much on a competitive basis. Whether it's the university you attend, the grades you get, the scores you receive, the wages you earn, your position on the job, or the games you play, competition is at the center, the very core of it all.

I enjoy the game of chess. I once played fairly regularly with a friend who was a fierce competitor. Under no circumstance could he stand losing, so the game could infuriate him. Fortunately for him, he was very good at it. He practiced criminal law the same way he played chess, which ought to tell you something if you ever need a good trial attorney.

I decided to help him overcome his problem with losing, so I gave him a deluxe computerized chess game. The game had a very fancy board and pieces and was designed for advanced players. I gave it to him for his birthday and insisted that he play and show me how it worked. In less than five minutes, I could see that my friend was much more likely to destroy this game than to learn to cope with losing.

I experience challenges playing a computer game called *Civilization*. I particularly like it, and I can get swallowed up in it. A day can zip by, and all I've managed to do is conquer a nation and take a much-needed and coveted resource. The idea of the game is to build a civilization from the very beginning, playing against other countries generated and managed by the computer. You can try to be peaceful, but even at the lower levels of the game, some other group will declare war on you and destroy you if they can. So you build armies, learn tactics and strategies, choose forms of government, and deal with unhappy citizens, just as in real life. I can tell you that it simply is not possible for me to play during fierce competition and maintain a coherent heart pattern, which suggests that the vicarious experience creates stress that's nevertheless real enough.

Why is it that competition, something apparently so pervasive in our lives, is almost synonymous with the emotions we place in the same category as anger, hostility, greed, and the like? Why is such striving stressful if it's supposed to be the natural way, which it must be, based on all of our existing survival models—ranging from theories of evolution to strategies designed by our Department of Defense? Is there a way to be truly competitive and not become emotionally attached or involved? If the answer turns out to be *yes,* is this what we really want?

There are environments today in which children compete but don't receive an accurate representation of their abilities. That is, everyone wins and gets a ribbon, toy, or some candy treasure. Many adults complain that this doesn't prepare kids for the real world, and the truth is, it doesn't.

Most of us are familiar with websites that auction merchandise, such as eBay, which have built an empire around competition. Usually even the novice bidder quickly develops a strategy to *win* and therefore pay the most money for an item. I know an attorney who finds bidding on the site almost addictive. He's always looking for some item of interest—not one he thinks of in advance but rather one he finds while searching the site. There can truly be a sense of pride and victory that comes from successfully executing a strategy and winning the prized object.

Competition in the marketplace isn't new. Businesses compete with each other, and that drives down prices. As consumers, we like the lowered figures. When the contest may cost us personally, however, perhaps because a company competes with our employer and we lose our job due to their low prices, there's a great outcry opposing "unfair" competition. After all, it might be argued, no one likes a bully.

Most nations have some sport that's a favorite, if not the official, pastime of the country. Indeed, it was the competition that we saw portrayed in John Carlin's book *Playing the Enemy: Nelson Mandela and the Game That Made a Nation* and in the movie *Invictus* that brought the nation of South Africa together. Nelson Mandela brilliantly used the sport of soccer to build national pride on the world stage, and this accomplishment had far-reaching domestic ramifications that assisted in unifying the country.

In America, football seems to have become king, but we have a love relationship with basketball and baseball as well, with sports like soccer gaining in popularity every year. We seem to highly treasure our athletes, and thus they're rewarded with huge salaries and bonuses. We also prize the corporate leaders of the world, especially if they're at all like Jack Welch and we own stock in General Electric. When someone like Welch or Lee Iacocca (one of the world's most successful businessmen) comes along, we recognize his value and want him rewarded. So we make the world even more competitive, for it's not just about gaining for customers; it's about competing for salary and position. We've all seen the movies portraying Wall Street and the activities that lead people to commit crimes in order to win and to commit suicide when they lose.

Real Competition Exists Within

What, then, is a balanced perspective? Should we try to take first place? Remember our earlier definition of winning as doing our very best? In my mind, the real competition exists within. When I redefine the game to examine myself against my top effort, there's no one to become upset with except me, myself, and

Competition

I. If I've done my best and work to improve steadily in every way, every day, then that's simply all there is.

This isn't some foolish idea but the only healthy way to view competition. The simple truth is that you'll never be satisfied with your performance if it's based on comparison to others. My dad used to tell me about fighting: "You may get a steak, but he'll get a hamburger while you're at it." Obviously, this statement was designed to remind me of the cost of conflict, for even when you win, you walk away hurt. There's always someone out there to knock you off your pedestal, unless the real challenger is yourself and you're doing your very best. That way, it's always win-win. You come in first because you do your very best, and you're a champion because this is what you compete for and who you strive against—yourself, your best.

Competition, then, need not be against someone else, and the highest form isn't war. General Patton was a brilliant military leader, but that didn't make him some guru of truth. Indeed, I'd argue that the real contest during battle is indeed with yourself. The general pointed at that when he implied that the test is really about how you deal with your inner decisions. If our duty is to our best, then I agree. Nothing advances your confidence about how you'll deal with competition until you make doing your best a habit—and then believing in yourself will eventually become purely academic.

Reflection

What do you think about competition? What would happen in your life if you stopped measuring yourself against others and simply raced with yourself—striving to do your very best regardless of whether you were already way ahead of the game or way behind? How would this attitude affect your life? Would you find peace in those areas where you're not the best? Would you soar to even greater heights in those areas where you are? Is this an idea worth trying?

CHAPTER 14

INSTINCT AND INTUITION

"I suspect we have internal senses. The mind's eye since Shakespeare's time has been proverbial: and we have also a mind's ear. To say nothing of dreams, one certainly can listen to one's own thoughts, and hear them, or believe that one hears them."

— AUGUSTUS WILLIAM HARE AND JULIUS CHARLES HARE

The human animal is an interesting species. We highly value our intellect and often discard our intuition and instinct. Our instincts have developed over billions of years, but because we often have very little intellectual understanding of each impulse as we experience it, we likely just totally relegate such signals to the back burners of premodern evolution. In other words, if we can't fully understand the impulse, then it must be an immature relic.

Anyone who's ever been around small children knows how easy it is for them to weep for seemingly endless periods when they lose their favorite toy, to say nothing of a pet. A broken car or doll, a dead goldfish or hamster—these are losses that every mom and dad dreads. Yet as parents, we often try to fix the situation with a new goldfish, doll, or hamster, or we substitute one animal for another.

"Why don't we get a small dog this time instead of a hamster? They're easier to take care of and they live much longer," we might suggest.

But when we do this, what are we really proposing? What's the unwritten subliminal message inherent in this kind of thinking?

One of my sons once drowned a chick. It was just a few days old, and he thought it was thirsty, so he took it to water and put its head in to drink. It was only there for a few seconds, but when he took the pressure off, it was dead. The little lifeless body drained all the color from my four-year-old son's face; when I discovered him sitting on the floor of the coop, he appeared almost in a state of shock.

Life can be very fragile, and we often learn that lesson when we're too young to fully understand it. Adults often compound the situation by offering a substitute message: Life is something that can be replaced. One dead hamster brings a new dog. Chickens? Well, they're cheap and plentiful, so don't worry about it—we'll just get a few more.

Lives of Quality

We learn very early to differentiate between lives of quality and those of little merit. In the process, we can dull our own awareness. Among our suppressed instincts and intuitions are sensibilities that address the value of all life. We have to be taught that Bambi really is fun to kill. We must learn that there's a renewable supply of pork, beef, chicken, and turkey, and that it just appears in the grocery store for our consumption.

An acquaintance of mine, whom I'll call John, had a successful career as a university professor and yet he harbored some deep insecurities for most of his life because his innocence was taken in this way. His story serves as a good example of my thoughts on lives of quality.

When John was just a boy of six or seven, his father brought home a baby goat. The animal lived in the enclosed front porch of their home for a few days before Easter. John played with the goat for hours each day. On Easter morning when John went out to the front porch, his new friend was gone. If you guessed that he found the goat on the supper table, you're correct. This was a life-haunting experience for him. Why?

Our instincts and intuitions inform us as children that animals can be our friends, that they have a special kind of intelligence, that we can communicate with them—albeit differently from the methods we use with other humans. Our education, however, teaches us that animals are different and further differentiates them into subcategories: these are pets; these are food; these are dangerous. Sometimes creatures fit into multiple categories, as did John's goat. They can be our companions, yet they can also end up on the table.

Is it immature to follow our instincts? If intuition suggests that we avoid someone or some place, is it smart to ignore the message and go with pure reasoning? When is it okay to recognize that those instincts constitute a viable channel for information?

How many subliminal messages, such as those extolling the virtues of a replacement dog for a lost hamster, have we used to dull our senses? What internal senses do we have that we can reliably depend upon?

It's said that we hear our self-talk, our mind chatter, almost all the time. Indeed, try to quiet your internal voice and see how many thoughts you have in spite of yourself and how much variety there is. This inner dialogue informs us of what we can do, what we wish to do, and what we think. It lets us know when we're overreaching and informs us when certain ideas are just wishful thinking. It's usually this same voice that utters the word *foolish* when we have a hunch, a feeling, or even an instinctual tendency toward or away from something. It's our very own internal talk that persuades us that our instincts and intuition are wrong, immature, or just silly. It is also what assures us that we're doing the right thing when we do listen to those feelings. What then is the difference?

My work and research informs me that the real distinction is all about what you want to think. Contemplate that, for it may be the most important item in this book. If you'd like to believe something, you almost certainly will accept any and all feelings, hunches, intuitions, and instincts that are in line with your accepted understanding.

Power of Suggestion

I used to show lie-detection examiners the power of suggestion. In fact, I've taught courses on countermeasures using hypnosis demonstrations as a strategy. One suggestion technique I employed began with taking a sheet of paper and writing a plus sign on one end and a minus on the other. I had a male subject come to the front of the class and suspend a simple pendulum over the paper, with the chain between his thumb and forefinger.

I explained that the ancient Egyptians used this method to divine the sex of unborn children by suspending it above the womb of an expectant mother. I continued by letting everyone know that if the subject was a male, the pendulum swung toward the plus; if a female, toward the negative. If I saw little movement after instructing my subject to concentrate on his sex, then I simply told him to say to himself, *I am a man*, to see if the pendulum responded accordingly.

I would add, "And if the pendulum fails to move, it means the subject is confused about his sexuality."

I must confess that this demonstration was conducted before it was a matter of political correctness to be sensitive to sexual preference per se. I assure you that the pendulum always moved, and it always agreed with the observed sex of the subject.

The bottom line is this: The power of suggestion created an expectation factor shared by a group (peers), and that generated a belief that led to the movement of the pendulum. Some of the individuals involved in these demonstrations swore up and down that they did nothing to influence the weight, but close observation tells us that muscle microtremors actually do the moving. Is this an example of the unconscious tending to the needs of the moment? This is, in fact, one way of seeing the matter.

Our beliefs absolutely predispose our findings in the real world. Not only is this true for ourselves but it can be true for others as well. Studies have shown that a teacher presented with a troubled, learning-impaired child and told that the child is very precocious and gifted but with some behavioral opportunities will produce a child that actually fits this description within a year.[1] (I prefer to say "behavioral opportunities" rather than "difficulties," as that terminology opens the door to the possibility of some benefit rather than being stuck in the struggle.)

Disconnect

Knowing that our inner voice is likely to tell us what we want to hear, when and where should we trust it? I believe that our instincts, hunches, intuitions, and even our dreams can be of great value as legitimate channels of information. I also believe that we must use a great deal of discretion when it comes to acting on this data. Trusting our inner guidance is something we all tend to want to do, but training it is something few actually undertake.

You can guide that inner voice to totally support all your ambitions. Indeed, I've spent a great deal of my life designing technology to do just that, and a number of solid scientific studies have demonstrated the effectiveness of this approach. Nonetheless, all the training in the world won't discount the fact that you have preferences, and whenever you're listening to your own inner guidance, you need to remember that it's biased.

Think of it this way: What would you tell your spouse if he or she chose an ugly outfit but was very pleased and proud about it? When my wife asks, "How do I look?" I already know the answer before I check it out. I'm not going to tell her something that would hurt her feelings!

With that understanding—and common sense confirms this—when an impulse tells me to be careful, and it comes from out of nowhere, I pay attention. When an inner voice tells me what I want to hear, I listen but recognize that I may be hearing only my own bias.

Why is that distinction important? What you believe truly matters, and believing in yourself is critical. But deciding when to listen to my intuition, my so-called instincts, my dreams, and my hunches—that becomes a critical matter of *discernment.*

The still, small voice within might be there to lead and protect, but what if we think we're hearing the inner voice when in reality we're hearing only what we want to hear. In other words, our goals and ambitions can cloud our minds so that it seems as though we're being guided when the message is really only a replay of what we want. We must learn to develop our minds and our understanding of ourselves before we can expect to get anything other than our existing beliefs back in this dialogue.

Indeed, I'd argue that it's imperative today to train our minds, to vigilantly choose what we put into them, and to exercise caution when it comes to relying upon what comes out of them. The old Socratic admonition asserts how useless an unexamined life is, and so it is with an unexamined mind. Washington Irving is reported to have summed it up this way: "Great minds have purposes; others have wishes."

Here is the real paradox: What you believe, your self-talk, and your inner channel of information control much of your reality.

They shape your expectations and thus your perceptions. In other words, ignoring that inner voice may well give rise to expecting the worst possible outcome instead of maintaining an optimistic viewpoint, and thus all the work to train your mind to feed back positive information can be cancelled. *And that doesn't work for your best!*

Invest in the Positive

I've learned from my own introspections and life experience, as well as from my work and research and that of others, that we should place our confidence in positive expectations, regardless of the doubt we may feel at the time. Perhaps we'll be disappointed and perhaps not. The fact of the matter is simple: Choose to invest your thinking in optimistic, confident thoughts, and you're much more likely to experience that reality than if you pursue the opposite. Self-doubt simply erodes the power of your belief, just as water seeping underneath a levee destroys its structure.

I find it helpful to actually conduct a dialogue with my inner self. I may sometimes ask a question regarding something I'm thinking about doing. For example, as I was working on this chapter, I awoke to several inches of new snow. When I asked myself about moving the horses to a safer area, my inner voice suggested that I do so. The reasons impressed me in the same way my intuition and hunches tend to do. Over the many years that I've done this, I've had some startling results. Not once do I remember a clear difference between my inner answer and the outer reality I lived. There have been ambiguities and disappointments, but never a response that was outright wrong.

Indeed, in my book *What Does That Mean? Exploring Mind, Meaning, and Mysteries,* I discussed this guidance and one of my disappointments. I was asked later during a radio interview whether or not I still listened to that internal voice. My answer was *yes.* You see, the question I'd asked had to do with my health, and I was told that I'd be fine and had nothing to worry about. Three days later, I had major surgery. I recovered just fine, however, and today I feel much stronger than before that event. Would it have been any help if my inner answer had been something such as, *Well, brace yourself, you're going to have to undergo major, life-threatening surgery—but don't sweat it—you'll be okay* . . . ? I don't think so.

I must add that all of us have a number of psychological mechanisms that might be called upon by a skeptic to explain both my use of the inner voice and the rational answer (rationalization) I just offered. But the bottom line is this: There's a possible explanation for everything we all do, and it's arguably based on some mechanic of the mind. Take your pick—choose to disbelieve the power of your own inner wisdom and put it all off on psychological mechanisms, or choose to try listening and test it for yourself.

Reflection

Intuition and instincts can guide you well, but only if you take the time to listen carefully and to sift out your biases and desires. This takes a great deal of honesty with yourself; but in the end, I guarantee that it will make such a positive difference in your life that you'll make *Believing in yourself always matters* your motto, too.

So what do you believe? Do you think it's immature to follow inner guidance? If not, when is it okay?

CHAPTER 15

AFTERLIFE AND END OF LIFE

"Death is not the greatest loss in life. The greatest loss is what dies inside us while we live."

— NORMAN COUSINS

You might think that a chapter on the end of life and the afterlife would be the last chapter in this book, but there's a definite reason why it isn't. There's been a lot of discussion in the political world today about so-called death panels. Under the administration of George W. Bush, the idea that the government would pay for end-of-life counseling became law. During the "Obamacare" health-care debate, it was suggested that this counseling be paid for every year as opposed to just once in a lifetime. Many conservative pundits immediately referred to this as constituting "death panels," suggesting that the purpose of the change was to allow health-care professionals to discourage expensive interventions for elderly citizens who had only a few more years to live anyway. According to the new bill, the physician would address this issue through the perspective of quality of life versus quantity of life. Dr. Tim Johnson of ABC News told Diane Sawyer that this was an adjustment doctors would be making in the future to accommodate the attitude of patients. So it's all about those receiving the care, one side will assert, and all about money, the other will argue.

My interest isn't with either point of view. There's something to giving the end-of-life process its due, as opposed to our historical attitude of pretending to ignore death or treating it as though it were a distant taboo—at least, when it comes to having a family discussion about the matter.

End-of-Life Discussion

Here's the issue: when should a family have this discussion—or should they even have it at all? What does it mean to sit down with your spouse and children and talk about your end-of-life options? Do you want to remain on artificial life support if the doctors determine you're in a permanent vegetative state? Or do you want the plug pulled? If your spouse or child wishes the latter for himself or herself, can you really agree to go through with it?

Recent research shows that doctors have made many mistakes about when a person is in a permanent vegetative state. In my book *What If?* this matter was one of the thought experiments. What if you discovered that many patients who were thought to be in such a vegetative state were, in fact, aware of everything going on around them? New discoveries have actually demonstrated this to be true.[1] Would you make the same decision for your loved ones that you'd make for yourself?

I believe in an afterlife and have discussed the hows and whys of that already in my book *What Does That Mean?* Any conversation about these topics should, of course, include your metaphysical perspective as well. Discussions about wills, estates, and related issues are fine, but they aren't truly the heart of the matter. What's particularly relevant, especially to your surviving loved ones, is how you feel about death.

Walter Scott said, "Death—the last sleep? No, it is the final awakening." A recent guest on one of my radio shows, August Goforth, sees the matter as *the risen*. Those who have crossed over have risen up out of the physical into a higher dimensional existence. *Goforth* is a pseudonym, and the man behind the name is more than just a writer. He's a licensed, practicing, and very successful psychotherapist who claims to speak to the risen every day. Obviously, if your family's view includes this kind of otherworld orientation, then your departure will be less traumatic than if their philosophy is "From dust thou art, and to dust you will return—gone—gone forever!" (You might think of this as just another reason, pragmatically speaking, for holding steadfastly to your belief in life after death.)

We need to know what the end-of-life discussion entails before we can determine if it's appropriate, and if it is, when. In order to make that determination, we must ask ourselves, *What other subjects should be considered in such a conversation?*

Sharing Your Philosophy

Your ideas about death are of supreme importance. Let's assume that you've covered your preferences about ending life in the event you're deemed to be in a permanent vegetative state, and you've fully discussed issues such as organ donations, wills, estates, and other legal matters. Now it's time to share your personal philosophy. What has living meant to you and why? What does your family mean to you and why? How would you like survivors to remember you? What are your regrets—relevant ones, such as failing to express your appreciation or affection as much as you could have?

This is a conversation you want to have before you're on your deathbed and emotions are high. Talk about death before something terminates your ability to address the issues. Leave your loved ones with the comfort that comes from knowing your thoughts. I want my family to know just how much I have enjoyed living, how much I have learned and continue to learn from life, how much love I have for them all, and just how close I'll always be. I add the words of Norman Vincent Peale: "I believe there are two sides to the phenomenon known as death, this side where we live, and the other side where we shall continue to live. Eternity does not start with death. We are in eternity now."

What we believe forms the grid upon which our end-of-life story is built. It's easy to see just how important what we believe is to others, especially those we care about. After all, the only thing we can really leave them that truly matters is the memory of our love and the example we lived.

Reflection

So what do you think about death and the afterlife? Have you discussed your beliefs with your loved ones? Do you think it's time to do so? You'll find that these conversations will add quality to your relationships and assist you in focusing on what's truly important in life.

CHAPTER 16

IT'S NEVER TOO LATE

"It is never too late to become what you might have been."
— ATTRIBUTED TO GEORGE ELIOT

What is too late? Great thinkers I admire have expressed their thoughts on this question. Elbert Hubbard, whose scrapbook I've enjoyed for some 30 years, said, "Everything comes too late for those who only wait." And Og Mandino, one of my favorite writers, said, "There is an immeasurable distance between late and too late."

What is this "immeasurable distance" and how does it relate to the idea of waiting until it's too late? *Distance* is actually a misnomer, for the idea is more one of time or action than of physical space. Think of it this way: If, on your deathbed, you truly forgive someone for something that you've held against him or her for a long time, that person is just as forgiven as he or she would have been many years earlier. As for the relationship that might have been shared with the individual who was forgiven—that's lost, at least in this lifetime, because you waited. How would you measure the distance between this deathbed scenario with dying bitter and unforgiving? Obviously, in a metaphor, there's a big difference between late and too late.

What would fall into the "too late" category if you died this hour? Have you ever thought of making a list—not a so-called bucket list about what you want to do, but a list that aims at making certain that those "too late" items are crossed off while you still have time? This can be tougher by far than the fun list of things you want to do before the proverbial curtain is drawn.

For many years, my life was much different than it is today. There was a time when nothing worked for me. I was suspicious, bitter, and angry and generally wore a chip on my shoulder. Many things changed me, and for that I'm eternally grateful! Still, to this day there are those for whom I hold no malice but who long ago relegated me to their "trash" heap. I often think about how to undo what has been done, and I always come to the same conclusion—it can't happen. What I *can* do is hold a special prayer in my heart and release any and all condemnation that I might harbor toward them and myself.

Forgive Yourself

One item that must be on your new "never too late" list is forgiveness. (Some may think at this point that it's too late for some things, but I'll clarify this a little later.) Often, you're chief among those needing this grace. Everyone makes mistakes; that's just the way it is.

My mother, like most moms, used to tell me that there's no sense crying over spilled milk. She was correct. The milk is gone, and no amount of lamentation will put it back in the container. I'm left with only two viable options: the first is to learn from my mistake, so that I'm more cautious in handling milk in the future; the second is to accept the forgiveness offered me by others and make sure I give it to myself.

For most of us, no one punishes us more than ourselves. It's easy to find the mind stuck circling some incident, statement, error, or injustice—whether done by ourselves or someone else—reliving it over and over. Instead of forgiving and letting go, we hang on and practice those negative feelings each time we think about the matter. Often, one upsetting event is only washed away by another; and in that way, we create a wider circle so that we can dwell upon all of the episodes collectively as well as individually. And once again, each time we recall any of them, we rehearse the emotion felt at the time.

It becomes quite obvious when explained in this light that you want not only to forgive immediately but also to let the matter go. If you're going to revisit past moments, reflect on good ones. In fact, research shows that just thinking about positive memories for 20 minutes a day strengthens the immune system. The fact that cycling through the unpleasant ones produces the opposite effect on the body shouldn't come as a surprise—that's just another good reason to let matters of this kind go.

Too Late

Okay, I can't put the milk back in the bottle—does that mean that it's too late? Once again, there might not be any hope for the milk, but that's not the case for you. Milk is an inanimate object. If we have injured human beings, they too have the ability to redeem the situation. In that case, we can make the effort, and then it's up to them to make the decision. The situation will be past saving only when we wait until our time on this plane has expired.

As I said earlier, there was a point in my life when I'd almost given up on myself. But the Universe hadn't, fortunately, and several circumstances moved me in a different direction. I tell this story in my book *Choices and Illusions*. Instead of repeating the story here, allow me to say just that "life sucks and then you die," or so my bumper sticker could have read in the past. One of the events that changed my life was a dream. It's a powerful metaphor, and it helped me. I'll share it with you in the hope that anyone who doubts his own right to redemption or who might think it's too late may enjoy the same liberating hope I was able to take away from the dream.

Once upon a time, a man looked to himself. He said himself, *I desire to serve God, but my life has been full of error. The example I have set is not that of a cleric. People will only scoff and say, "Know ye them by their fruits." Who am I, then, to speak for or of God?*

With these words circling within his head, the troubled man lay down to rest. He spoke to God: "Your will, not mine, be done."

As he drifted into sleep, pictures began appearing that told this story:

Once there stood a tree—a tree of life, full of fruit. The limbs bent toward the earth under the weight of lush red cherries. The cherries danced in jubilee with the breeze that bathed their tender skins and turned their fullness and vivid color to face the Father, the Sun of the heavens.

With the dew and the rain, they polished their beauty and drank of the earth, to store within the energy and vitality of life taken from the soil through the roots and fired with the spirit of the Sun radiating through the leaves of their parent tree.

But alas, not all of the children of the tree would mature into lush red fruit. Out of an urge to experience and learn on his own, one turned away from the Father and ignored the parental warnings. Charlie, as he was known by the others, kept his life juices warm, daring the cold, the frost, the elements. He began to fill with color and mature early.

Pivoting on his base, he turned away from the Sun and took shade in the leaves. Daring to fornicate with the world, Charlie refused to release the natural pesticides within himself and took up affairs with the parasites.

Soon his delicate skin was broken, and his fruit exposed. The fragrance attracted the birds, and they too feasted on his flesh. Charlie lived off the flesh and of the world. Passion, experience, and knowledge were his prize.

Then one day, the gardener came. Gently, he took from the parent the pure and ripened children, leaving only Charlie behind. Hanging alone, Charlie looked about him. The fall nights were cold and lonely. His friends, the birds, were on the wing, abandoning him. His flesh had spoiled, and even the insects avoided him now. His soul hung onto his tattered body. The elements he'd once faced with a thrill now threatened to snap him from the stem of life. Charlie was sad and lonely. He'd learned these things: knowledge is not necessarily wisdom, experience is not always a kind teacher, and passion is sometimes a poison that betrays whatever value there is to be had in experience and knowledge.

Charlie looked up at the beautiful blue sky and the buoyant white billowy clouds adrift, seemingly with nothing to do nor a care in the world, lazily sailing across the vast blue heavens. *They and the lilies of the field,* Charlie said to himself.

"Dear God," he spoke aloud, "I have sinned. I have wasted the beauty of your flower and turned my back on simple truth. In my pursuit of wisdom, I lost sight of Your Great Form and indulged in physical illusions. I was lost. I alone am to blame. I give my essence over to thee, Creator of all that is good within me and all that could ever be love within me. For you are Eternal Love, and what is best for me is also your way. That I should discover this so late in my life is my most significant regret.

"I have watched the caterpillar spin his cocoon and perch on the leaves above me as a butterfly," Charlie continued, "but I fear that this recognition has come so late in my life that I will be unable to share this Beauty, this Truth, with others."

With that Charlie lowered his head. Suddenly a squirrel jerked him from the limb and scampered down the tree and across the meadow. The squirrel paused, examined Charlie, and then, as though rejecting him, dropped Charlie in the grass.

Charlie rested there for a day or two, and then the snow came. Covered by the white blanket, Charlie slept.

The seasons passed as though in the twinkling of an eye. Charlie took root and grew strong. From his branches came blossoms, followed by fruit more beautiful than Charlie could ever remember beholding.

Charlie praised and gave thanks to God!

The lowly man in my dream raised his head from slumber. His prayer had been answered. The Lord does not forsake man; man forsakes the Lord. Thy will, not mine, be done; for, after all, in their eternal boundless beauty, they are one and the same.

The Next Step

The courage to change your life is a process, one step at a time. The wisdom required to take that action rests within all of us. With every step we take, our confidence increases and we realize the true power of the gift of life. In this process, we find that believing in ourselves unlocks so much magic that life takes on an entirely new glorious nature.

Joseph Campbell tells a story about Friedrich Nietzsche that's instructive to us all:

At a certain moment in Nietzsche's life, the idea came to him of what he called "the love of your fate." Whatever your fate is, whatever the heck happens, you say, "This is what I need." It may look like a wreck, but go at it as though it were an opportunity, a challenge.

If you bring love to that moment—not discouragement—you will find the strength is there. Any disaster that you can survive is an improvement in your character, your stature, and your life. What a privilege! This is when the spontaneity of your own nature will have a chance to flow. Then, when looking back at your life, you will see that the moments which seemed to be great failures followed by wreckage were the incidents that shaped the life you have now. You'll see that this is really true.

Nothing can happen to you that is not positive. Even though it looks and feels at the moment like a negative crisis, it is not.[1]

Reflection

It may sound a little morbid, but think of yourself on your deathbed. From that vantage point, look back at your life. Is there anything you'd change? Are there things that previously seemed really important but that just don't matter from this perspective? What can you do today that would shift this scene and reduce or eliminate the regrets? Which relationships can you heal? Which ones will you decide are best left alone? Can you find the silver lining to the "bad" events? How can you make sure that you fully benefited from your entire journey—the good parts and the unpleasant ones? When you can look back at the negative events and say that you wouldn't change anything, since without them you wouldn't be the person you are today, then you'll know that you've succeeded.

What can you do today that will highlight your glorious contribution to the miracle of life? What is it that you believe, and how does that matter?

CHAPTER 17

BALANCE

"The mind of the perfect man looks like
a mirror—something that doesn't lean forward or
backward in its response to the world. It responds
to the world but conceals nothing of its own. Therefore
it is able to deal with the world without suffering pain."

— CHUANG TZU

Balance is one of the most difficult things to acquire and maintain. The ability to be in the world but not of it takes some doing.
It's one thing to lay claim to this feat, and quite another to remain
there. For example, I know several gifted individuals whom many
regard as gurus. Not one of them is able to remain balanced 24/7,

and a significant number have acted on at least one occasion in a manner that totally contradicts their teachings.

There are subtle differences between balance and being unattached. On the surface, some might think they're synonymous. Sometimes, however, the latter can take on the flavor of aloofness or even a certain dispassionate air. It may be that we need balance in our unattached philosophy. For example, you may do your best and be quite certain that you're uncommitted to the outcome, only to find that your efforts result in nasty stimuli that threaten or challenge you. Maintaining equilibrium at times like that can be a tool to sustain our intention of detachment.

What I've found is that there are prods and pokers that will knock most of us off our high horse, as my mother used to say. For some, it's a threat to the pocketbook, for others, the ego, their loved ones, or some other trigger. We all have our Achilles' heel, our soft spots. I've also learned that someone close to us has the handle on the poker and jabs us from time to time, just to remind us that our balance is not yet perfected. What's more, this is as it should be, for it not only keeps us humble but provides the test material for the next exam.

Fear

Life is a schoolyard, and your teachers are often those who perturb you most. When someone irks you, pay attention. This is a good habit to acquire because you'll systematically begin to discover the hows and whys that underpin your reactions. Most often, you're likely to discover that the trigger is based in fear. Here are a few issues that typically underlie this response:

— Fear of loss: Perhaps you have your security wrapped up in financial matters or perhaps it's an issue with your ego—somehow it's about to be damaged, for you'll be made to look stupid or small. We all have security concerns. The threat of the loss of something important to us invariably triggers this.

Balance

— Fear of separation from a loved one: Jealousy and some forms of competitiveness are linked deeply to our need to be cared for. It's not uncommon for that need to be rooted in such beliefs as *I'm the best possible person for this individual,* or *He loves me because I'm special to him.* There are many more such ideas, but these two make my point. It's easy to think of our loved one's rejection as being in favor of someone else, which insults our view that we're the chosen one. Someone else is now somehow superior, and this is as damaging to our self view as any other aspect of the separation.

— Fear of exposure: Perhaps there's a yarn that we've spun or a misdeed that we fear will become public. This threat can provoke the strongest response.

I could go on, but each and every one comes back to fear. In other words, fear is our private "Enemy Number One." Fear is the lever that pries us off balance. It's the trigger that provokes those unwanted reactions that can lead to the incidents we need to clear from our "never too late" list. This dread is the foundation of so many negative emotions that I believe all of them spring from some version of it.

To find balance, we must dispose of fear. We must release our conditional agreements and expectations, trusting in Divine will. Consciously choosing to spend time forgiving and letting go is the best way I know of to banish this specter. Pardoning others does the trick because it removes expectation. When I forgive and turn the matter over to the will of God, there's nothing remaining to be afraid of. Whatever will be, will be.

Fear arises as a result of my expectation. I become terrified that I might fail, be rejected, be penalized, or be deprived. Or perhaps I'm worried that I might be exposed, lose, win, and on and on. This anxiety is a conditional state built upon the foundation of anticipation. It holds within itself a punishment-reward scheme, and when I grant clemency to myself and all others, turning everything over, fear dissipates, for there are no longer any expectations.

Forgiveness requires a certain trust. It means having faith that there's a reason to let things go, a purpose, and this faith ultimately gives rise to accepting a higher order of affairs. This is the true power of the process, and it removes blame. This, in turn, restores our ability to move forward. Each time we forgive, we become more open to allowing ourselves to be wrong and make mistakes, and in this way we grow mentally and spiritually. Our judgment becomes wiser, and our overreactions disappear. In time, we gain the ability to see ourselves as being in the world but not of it, for like Chuang Tzu's mirror, we understand our role, our power, and our limitations.

Balance will come when we live free of fear and are therefore unattached to the outcome, confident in the will of the Divine. Balance is achievable when we forgive, let go, and accept our own redemption. We do deserve that grace for, like the story of the prodigal son in the Bible, our Creator has already forgiven us, and this forgiveness becomes tangible just as soon as we acknowledge our error.

Reflection

Fear undergirds the structure of your self-imposed limitations. The antidote is forgiveness—of yourself and of others. What do you need to pardon? When you start looking at this issue, you'll find more and more incidents—many that you thought you'd forgotten. Take some time every night before going to sleep to reflect on your relationships with others and with yourself and make a conscious effort to forgive and let go. I promise you that this one exercise will cause a quantum jump in your spiritual journey.

The importance of forgiving and letting go has been one of the cornerstones of my teaching for more than 20 years. I believe this principle to be so important for the individual and the world at large that about 15 years ago I took one of my best-selling InnerTalk subliminal programs, *Forgiving and Letting Go,* and made it available free of charge. (InnerTalk is a patented technology that has been researched by numerous major universities and been found effective at priming self-talk and thereby changing behavior.) You can get your copy by going to **www.eldontaylor.com** and clicking on *forgiveness*.

CHAPTER 18

WHAT'S WRONG WITH THIS PICTURE? THE LAW OF ATTRACTION

"There are no easy answers, but there are simple answers."
— RONALD REAGAN

Imagine a child, perhaps your own. Let's say his name is Bobby, and he wants very badly to win the state competition in an event—for example, a "Math Is Cool" competition. Bobby is good at math, really good. He practices and studies for the upcoming tournament. He hears about visualization, so he begins picturing the victory.

Bobby reads all about visualizing success. He reads books that teach the power of attraction, the power of the mind to create, the power to focus and visualize in detail and with emotion, and to let the image go, knowing that it's done. The boy has done all of this, and he's done it just exactly as he was taught.

Bobby does well at state, but he doesn't win—he doesn't even get an award. He goes away sad and feeling broken. Bobby knows the winner. The other kid didn't practice, study, or visualize. In fact, he didn't even seem to care if he won or not. Bobby doesn't understand and comes to you for answers. What do you tell him?

Pause now and genuinely reflect on this. What would you tell Bobby? What would you tell your own child?

What's wrong with this picture? Take a moment and ask yourself this question again: *What's wrong with this picture?*

I assume that before you continue reading, you've taken the time to give serious thought to the preceding paragraphs. If not, please do so, for the value here isn't in how quickly you can read the material or whether you comprehend the words; it's in the feeling that comes when you realize that what's wrong is beyond your control. Perhaps it's also easy to become agitated—maybe this visualization stuff is all just so much hocus-pocus.

Visualization

Here's what we know scientifically about visualization: it works to improve motor skills. Vividly imagining shooting free throws with a basketball is statistically almost as effective as practicing. Visualization can also work to attract things into people's lives. It can influence how they walk, dress, speak, and even how they talk to themselves. It can definitely influence levels of confidence, form self-fulfilling prophecies, and mold expectations while shaping futures and careers in some ways. But does it create, as in painting a picture or building a race car? Even more provocative a question is this: *Should we be visualizing the stuff we want to create?*

On any given night in America, a million people might be tuned in to some lottery drawing, all hoping to win the jackpot. If they all vividly visualize their numbers being drawn, will the prize be split or will it take one million episodes for each to realize the dream? When put in this light, when held under this level of scrutiny, what's real about manifestation as spelled out in primers like *The Secret,* where visualization is the pathway to manifestation—ask, believe, receive?

In my opinion, there's a lot of nonsense out there about visualization. We're all capable of certain types of creation; but according to my training and experience, in order for a lasting manifestation to be realized, we must first make changes in ourselves. We're much more likely to manifest success when we look and act successful. Creating a vision board and hanging it in the family room next to that good old TV; filling the board with pictures of the house, the car, and the flower garden of our dreams; visualizing these things over and over; even mentally smelling the flowers, feeling the leather seats, or holding the doorknob, then opening our eyes and watching that television while we relax and eat—that just doesn't cut it!

In other words, if the changes occur within us, then the manifestation may follow. But then we must ask the question, *Just because we can, should we?* This reminds me of a story I like about a man who finds God:

> God looks upon this man as a parent might its child. Anxious to tell the child a few things, he approaches to speak. There are only a few brief moments available, for God knows that soon this interlude will disappear. Before the Creator can speak, however, the man, recognizing the Divine presence, anxiously begins an endless stream of questions. Like a child's, they're queries such as "Why is the sky blue?" and "Why is the earth round?" God patiently provides the answers, but suddenly the phone rings and

our man is awakened. *Wow,* he thinks, *God just answered my questions in my dream.*

Unfortunately, the thing he didn't ask would have given God a chance to tell our fellow just exactly what he wanted to impart. The unasked question was, *What do you want me to know now, God?*

Isn't visualization a little along this line if what we're doing is designed to fulfill us, to serve our purpose—for that matter, to make us truly happy? Should Bobby have been asking, *What would you have me know and do now?* as opposed to attempting to force an outcome?

I submit that each of us is different, with unique gifts and separate identities, and all of this is part of our birthright. It's in accepting those gifts and employing them to the very best of our ability that we fulfill our purpose. My friend and wife says, "Let me know what you want me to know and do. Let me do Thy work, and if I'm doing as I should be doing, help me so that it's easy." I think of it this way: "Let me do Thy will, for my perfect will is Thy will."

Consistency matters. We can visualize improvement, we can even see our personal success, but then releasing that image with the words *This or something better, according to the highest good of all concerned,* will ensure that our efforts don't end in disappointments.

Reflection

What do you think about the law of attraction and the ability to simply visualize success? Have you ever tried visualization and failed? If so, did you attempt to discover why that result was in your best interest? On the other hand, did you succeed only to realize that you didn't want it after all? What would happen if, rather than working on creating the outcome you want, you ask for guidance to do the best thing for all concerned? Try it, and let me know what happens.

CHAPTER 19

FROLIC AND FOLLY

*"The life of the folly is empty of gratitude, full of anxiety,
all of it focused in the ghosts of the future."*

— EPICURUS

I'm a great believer in enjoying life! I'm also a strong believer in a good work ethic, and I see nothing wrong with the idea of working hard. To some nowadays, work is equivalent to a swear word. Indeed, we seem to live at a time when entitlement has taken the place of self-reliance. Over the years, I've received at least a dozen or more letters from people who have written to condemn my use of the word *work*. They insist that it's a bad word.

Think about how the word work is used—such as work out, work up to, or working model. Remember it as a synonym for a job, as in, "Have you found work yet?" Then, of course, there are such uses as the works of a Creator or other works of wonder by both men and their gods. There's the work of nature and of an artist, but I suspect the use that's most objected to has to do with the concept of toil.

I would suggest that the word is only objectionable to those who've never learned the joy of good, old-fashioned hard work. Perhaps that brings images of toil. "By the sweat of my brow" metaphors may pop into mind. But even this, when performed with an attitude of joy, becomes the opposite of the same activity when it's begrudged.

"What do you mean, the joy of work?" some might ask. And again, I'd emphatically say, "*Joy!*" *Work* isn't a negative word. Webster defines this usage as follows:

> Activity in which one exerts strength or faculties to do or perform something: *a :* sustained physical or mental effort to overcome obstacles and achieve an objective or result *b :* the labor, task, or duty that is one's accustomed means of livelihood *c :* a specific task, duty, function, or assignment often being a part or phase of some larger activity

Two of the programs that I developed using my patented InnerTalk method are entitled *Joy of Work* and *Prosperity and Abundance*. Both of these programs contain affirmations such as *I work hard*. This is the usage that my critics assert is negative.

Working Hard

I work hard almost every day. Not that it's always difficult, nor does it have a tough surface, but it's hard in the sense that I can become so immersed in it that the outside world disappears. I labor in my barn with my horses, and the sweat of my brow literally pours. I enjoy that. It's a good workout; and when it's finished, I have a great sense of satisfaction and accomplishment.

When I was a young man and wanted to find a job, a family friend took me aside to offer some advice. He was successful, so I listened and took his words to heart. He suggested that whenever I applied, I should make it clear that whatever the position was, it was the one I most wanted. So when I went to a shoe store, I told the owner that I really wanted to learn the shoe business and that's why I was applying. In other words, I wasn't just shopping around for any old job, going from one place to another and leaving my application—no, instead, I'd chosen this one!

This friend also told me that whenever I was employed, I should do my very best, really show interest and energy, and set myself apart by my willingness to demonstrate that I genuinely loved to work. He said that if I did this, I'd never want for work, and he was right. Many times in my life, former employers have tried to get me back. I never had trouble finding a job. This is the advice I give my children to this day, only at this point from the perspective of an employer. And now, more than ever, I can see the value behind this approach.

There's a crowd today that tends to think they can just visualize everything without having to soil their hands or toil until the sweat flows. Work is beneath them. The idea of immersing themselves in their work, even if it's at a desk, is also foreign. The workplace is where they go until something better comes along, and it's where they're entitled to certain rights and benefits. And this is precisely the attitude that drives jobs abroad and leads to outsourcing—it isn't just the higher costs of a payroll in this country; it's the lack of appreciation and productivity.

Dedicating Your Best

Hard work is the ability to dedicate your very best to whatever the job might be. Your best is never divided by nine other simultaneous interests or diluted by lazily meandering from place to place, taking your time to do whatever your task is. Indeed, your position comes with certain duties or a job description. *Duty* is a good word, too. There's duty to country and loved ones, and that includes yourself. You can't perform your duty by cheating anyone, which is exactly what you do when your effort is less than your best.

It's folly to believe that loafing, doing as little as possible, or doing only what's asked of you will lead to anything other than more of the same. In fact, I think it's foolish to provide unemployment compensation to those who are fully capable of working while not requiring them to work on some project that could contribute to the civic good. Let me give you an example. Not long ago, I had a 4,000-square-foot building constructed. The structure wasn't complete when winter came, and the crew pulled off the job. They did everything they realistically could, but then they went home and collected unemployment for three months. This was a team of first-rate builders. Why not put them to work repairing and rebuilding for the community? Let them be paid for their unemployment while they use their labor and tools for the town. Prison inmates are worked in this way, so why not the capable people who are on the dole?

Not long ago, I was in a Walmart looking for kits to build gingerbread houses. I asked one clerk for help, and he pointed off toward the other end of the store, muttering, "On the candy aisle, if we have any." Once at that end of the store, I asked a second clerk, and he said that the product must be sold out but that it had been displayed on an end cap.

Because no one had directed us toward any end cap, while my wife searched one aisle after another on the grocery side, I found another person to ask. This time it was a very pleasant young woman. Unlike the gruff "I'm too busy for you" answers that I'd been getting, she informed me that on that very morning, she'd walked through the store before she began work to see what products had changed, where things had been moved, what was on sale, and so forth. She'd noticed the gingerbread-house kits, so if I followed her, she'd take me to them. I called out to my wife, and off we went.

We walked back to the other end of this *supersized* store, and there on an end cap were the kits. I thanked the clerk and told her how pleasant it was to have her assistance. I further contrasted her help to that of the two men I'd asked earlier, and she immediately defended her employer by saying that Walmart policy didn't permit pointing and the like and that salespeople were trained to lead their customers to the product and to answer questions honestly.

Obviously, this young woman was both a breath of fresh air and an example of the advice I'd been given as a young man. On her own time, she had checked out the store. She went the extra mile, and she was a role model for fellow employees. Unfortunately, I failed to get her name so that I could later write to her employer. Perhaps one day she'll hear of her story in this book and know just how much she was appreciated and admired for doing her work so well!

Time to Work—Time to Play

There's a child's story that addresses how important it is to always do your best, even when it seems that your efforts may be futile:

> There were two friends named Tom and Jerry. They both needed jobs, so they approached a merchant who gave them each a wicker basket and took them down to a well. He instructed them to draw water from the well in the wicker baskets all day and then left. Tom thought this was foolish, so he took a nap. After all, the water just ran through the baskets. Jerry did as he was told, faithfully drawing water for hours. At the end of the day, he noticed that there were small gold nuggets in the basket, so he took them to the merchant. Jerry was given a job and rewarded for his work. Tom left, embarrassed.

The moral of this kid's story is one that many adults have yet to learn. I believe that we all have the ability to do our best.

Sometimes this means following instructions. There's a time for frolic and a time for toil. I believe that playing hard is fun and so is working hard. Both have their rewards and their joys. It's foolish to think that good luck follows selfish laziness. The folly of our time is to think that we're entitled to more than the opportunity to do our utmost. I believe that everyone has a right to pursue happiness, so long as individual delight doesn't come at the expense of others. When we let ourselves down, we let everyone down.

So once again, work hard and play hard, and life will bring you great rewards. I was once told that I must have two rabbit ears behind both of my own ears because I was so lucky. I truly believe that old trite but true axiom: *The harder you work, the luckier you become!*

Reflection

What are your views on this subject? Do you believe that working hard is something you shouldn't have to do, especially in a world of abundance? If so, how is this kind of thinking panning out for you? If it hasn't brought you what you want, do you attribute this only to your lack of ability to manifest things? If you thought of hard work in the same category as play—or if you took this further and thought of all labor as Divine service—how would you feel? It's possible that if you decided to take a sense of joy and gratitude to your place of work, if you did your utmost best, if you not only did what you were asked but went the extra mile as well, that appreciation and even financial reward would naturally follow. What do you think?

CHAPTER 20

BLESSINGS AND RESOLUTIONS

"A man without ambition is dead. A man with ambition but no love is dead. A man with ambition and love for his blessings here on earth is ever so alive."

— **PEARL BAILEY**

Not too long ago, another Christmas came and went. I remember sitting back on that holiday after spending about six hours in the kitchen with my lovely wife, patting my stomach, and realizing that once again I'd eaten a little more than was comfortable. I thought to myself just how blessed most of us are.

I BELIEVE

I happened to mention to my wife a thought that had just come across my mind: love is the great equalizer. I've met so many people who are much less fortunate than I, yet most of them are happy. Their contentment rests in the love they share with another. If you give this a little thought, then you realize just how important your dear ones are.

One of my fondest Christmas memories happened many years ago when I was cohosting a radio show with Jim Kirkwood called *The Good News Hour.* We decided to do something extra special one year, so we worked up a volunteer army of helpers from our listeners to feed the largest homeless shelter in Salt Lake City. I called upon such merchants as Sears to donate stockings, gloves, hats, and the like so that we could give every indigent a gift. I spoke to local grocers, who donated turkeys, stuffing, pies, and other food for the dinner. Our radio fans did the cooking, and as an extra, I asked my friend Duane Sutherland, who was chief of police for South Jordan, Utah, for his help. Duane spoke with his staff, and as a result, most of them volunteered to come serve the meals, refill the drinks, and pass out the gifts.

On the evening of our Christmas meal, the press showed up to film the event ("news at 10" stuff). There were some 100 hungry and cold homeless people and nearly the entire South Jordan police department in uniform (no guns). It was a special kind of bonding experience for everyone. The facility didn't have enough tables to seat everyone, so many just sat on the floor. Officers passed among them, refreshing their drinks, delivering gifts, and serving second helpings.

At one point, about an hour in, one great big lumberjack sort of fellow stood up. He asked to speak, and of course I said *yes.* In a broken voice, he told of how he'd hated police because he seemed to always be at odds with them, yet here they were serving him as though he were important. The tears began to flow, and he sobbed out the rest of his statement. He could no longer hate cops, and he was so very sorry for ever doing so.

The silence from the crowd while this big man spoke was incredible, and then the chorus of *Yeahs!* that followed was almost in perfect harmony. More than one of us was moved enough that we had to turn our heads to dry our eyes before looking at each other. It was a precious time that I'll never forget, and neither will the other individuals who were there.

Service

It shouldn't take a holiday for us to remember to be grateful or a new year to inspire resolutions. I resolve right now—and I do this every morning—to turn up my efforts at helping others. I want many more of the warm, fuzzy moments that come when I know my life has made a difference to someone.

I invite you to take the challenge and turn up your efforts as well. I believe that the world improves one person at a time, but collectively we possess a power that's much more than the sum of its parts. I believe that paramount to character is an identity that incorporates our fellow human beings as an extension of ourselves. As the poet John Donne put it, "Never send to know for whom the bell tolls; for it tolls for thee." Not only could the misfortunes of others today be your lot tomorrow but in an interconnected sense they're losses to you now.

I believe in helping others help themselves, and I know that in doing so, we improve our own lives as well. One may wear a bell so the blind horse can find his way, but what would life be like if there were no companion to give such aid? If you've ever felt lonely, separated from the rest, or cut off from the herd, so to speak, then volunteer at a homeless center, hospice, meal or mentoring program, or . . . I could go on and on, for there are many places that need you. In giving of yourself, you'll find that you're never again alone. As Martin Luther King, Jr., so aptly put it:

> Everybody can be great, because anybody can serve. You don't have to have a college degree to serve. You don't have to make your subject and your verb agree to serve . . . You don't have to know the second theory of thermodynamics in physics to serve. You only need a heart full of grace. A soul generated by love.[1]

Reflection

Do you believe that love is the great equalizer? We often receive our greatest blessings in what we give. Our highest purpose is probably in how we serve. Why don't you try this for yourself, if you haven't already?

CHAPTER 21

FALSOPHRENIA

*"It behooves us to strip away all our prejudices and
seek out a friend of God. However, when we've spent our
whole life in the company of people who lack discrimination,
then our own discriminative faculty becomes weak, and
that true friend may pass us by unrecognized."*

— ATTRIBUTED TO MEISTER ECKHART

We live in an interesting time and in a polarized world where
things can seem black and white. In theory, many issues can seem
to be clear—this is wrong, and that's right. But the practical implications are frequently not as clearly defined, which can lead to
confusion. Indeed, things are more often shades of gray; and more

and more people get the feeling that it's a "damned if you do, and damned if you don't" world that we live in. Why is that? It would be easy at this point to launch into a discussion about political or religious differences, but that would be looking outward when, in my view, we should always first look inward.

Soul-searching, as it has been called, is all about an inner examination of motives and beliefs. The very term presupposes at least two things. First, we have the ability to evaluate ourselves. Second, we're somehow capable of being dishonest with ourselves at a level beneath the surface of what we think of as ordinary consciousness.

Lying to ourselves at an unconscious level is something I think of as "falsophrenia." This condition is pandemic today, especially in the United States and other highly developed countries. I derived the word from these roots:

- *False,* in the sense that we aren't in touch with our authentic selves

- *Phrenic,* in the sense that this is purely an issue that arises from how we manage our minds

Some of the symptoms of falsophrenia include holding two mutually exclusive values or beliefs and either being unaware of the discrepancy or inventing arguments to justify or rationalize it. Another symptom can be seen as an escape mechanism: I'm feeling so out of balance and lost that I need to immerse myself in distractions such as shopping, watching TV, drinking, and eating. There are, of course, many other symptoms, but I think you get the picture.

Media-ocracy

We live in a "media-ocracy" today. Governments around the world use the media to manage their message. Print and digital outlets seek to own your thoughts, desires, and ambitions. That is the case whether we're talking about video news releases (VNRs)

aimed at winning the minds and hearts of the audience and produced by government agencies with the aid of psychological op-
erations or about a local retail commercial designed to promote
consumption. Buying things, after all, is the engine of our economy. It feels good to shop; shopping relieves stress and anxiety; and
goods such as fancy cars and clothes define us.

With all of these overt attempts to manipulate our psyche,
what are aware people to do? Should we throw our hands in the air
in frustration? That would be the easy thing, a Pontius Pilate action, an "it's on you, not on me" attitude. Should we scream about
all of the things that simply aren't right? Should we just complain
to those who will listen?

Power of One

I believe there are two things we must all do. The first is, of
course, to pay attention and spend some time every day thinking about what we do and why we do it. Are our opinions simply
following the popular views of the day? After all, it feels better to
agree and belong than to disagree and be all alone.

Whatever your values are, spend some time exploring the opposite perspective. Are there any points that you do agree with?
Why do "they" think and feel the way they do? Is there any value
in their ideas? It's only by doing this that you can be certain your
beliefs truly are your own. Just remember, though, that everyone
has an agenda to foist upon you, and it's up to you to sort it all out.

The other way to discover who you are is by learning about
your worth. In my mind, the best way to do so is by helping others. As I discussed in the last chapter, serving others may be our
highest purpose. When you go to the aid of someone in need, you
quickly realize two things. First, it feels good. Second, you're important—you make a difference. If just to one other human being,
you mean something! Think about it. What else makes you feel
better or more fully realize the power of one?

What is the power of one? I was recently interviewed by radio host Steve Maraboli. He and I share an idea that surprised me when I heard him voice it. He simply refers to this as *the power of one*—one good deed, one kind act, one smile, one caring action, one person transforming the world, one person at a time.

If we want the world to change, we need to change. We must become what it is that we seek. We lead by example. People are creatures of imitation. Behavior is contagious, and that's why the past has seen hysterical illness spread, vigilantes carry out atrocities, and honest people look the other way while someone is brutally raped or killed.

Nothing Changes until You Do

I believe in the vast, unlimited potential for good that resides within every human being. It may lie dormant for a lifetime, but it's never too late to raise it up. The person who at 80 risks everything to save one drowning child—the first good thing he's done in his entire life—may just have rescued the one who will save the world. There are lots of true stories about the person who saves someone only for that individual to later come to the aid of a loved one of the original rescuer. It's truly never too late—but then, I've said that before, haven't I? What I *haven't* yet discussed regarding the subject is this: nothing changes until you do.

Living falsely to ourselves not only corrupts our true potential but makes us doubly susceptible to being controlled. Sometimes we're the manipulators, intent on preserving our image of self. I like the way Richard Rohr states the matter in his book *Everything Belongs*:

> Our false self is who we think we are. It is our mental self-image and social agreement, which most people spend their whole lives living up to—or down to. It is all a fictional creation. It will die when we die. . . . It is endlessly fragile, needy, and insecure, and it is what we are largely dealing with in the secular West.

The false self is inherently needy because it has no metaphysical substance whatsoever. It is formed entirely in psychological and mental time and changes or dies easily. Yet most people spend their entire lives projecting, protecting, and maintaining this fiction.

The true self is indestructible and characterized by an inner abundance. It is not needy, easily offended, or hurt. The true self is characterized by contentment, an abiding low-level peace and happiness, although now and then it becomes pure joy. It knows that *all* is ok—despite it all![1]

Artificial Life

An interesting piece of research suggests just how easy it is to construct a false self in ways most of us wouldn't think of. Reporting in *Psychological Science*, Gerald Echterhoff of Jacobs University–Bremen tells us how a team of psychological scientists discovered that watching others' actions can lead to false memories of self-performance. Subjects viewed a video of someone else shuffling cards, shaking a bottle, or some other simple action. They were also asked to perform a number of simple actions but not those they saw in the video. They then reported performing the action shown in the video when asked about it two weeks later.

Simply watching video while performing other simple tasks on demand appears to give rise to the mind incorporating the memory of the viewed action with the memory of the actual action. Living as we do in a technological world, how much of what we see becomes incorporated in our own memories and belief systems? The ramifications here are immense—video games, reality TV, and horror movies—all sculpting who we are!

Phineas Gage

In some senses, as I suggested in my book *What If?*, we live in a world very much like a simulator. Arguably, you and I are what artificial-intelligence folks call "a-lifes," or artificial life. Our program is written in our brains and environment. Our minds are wired to produce our experiences, feelings, dispositions, moods, and even religious experiences. The famous case of Phineas Gage illustrates just how much of who we are is hardwired in the brain.

Gage was a railroad worker who survived a horrendous accident with a tamping iron that penetrated his brain. The accident destroyed much of his left frontal lobe. Before the accident, he was a responsible foreman for the railroad and had an admirable temperament. But he was a changed man following the accident. According to his first attending physician, Dr. John Martyn Harlow:

> The equilibrium or balance, so to speak, between his intellectual faculties and animal propensities, seems to have been destroyed. He is fitful, irreverent, indulging at times in the grossest profanity (which was not previously his custom), manifesting but little deference for his fellows, impatient of restraint or advice when it conflicts with his desires, at times pertinaciously obstinate, yet capricious and vacillating, devising many plans of future operations, which are no sooner arranged than they are abandoned in turn for others appearing more feasible. A child in his intellectual capacity and manifestations, he has the animal passions of a strong man. Previous to his injury, although untrained in the schools, he possessed a well-balanced mind, and was looked upon by those who knew him as a shrewd, smart businessman, very energetic and persistent in executing all his plans of operation. In this regard his mind was radically changed, so decidedly that his friends and acquaintances said he was "no longer Gage."[2]

The Spiritual Brain

The more we learn about the brain, the more we discover that our every experience, sensation, feeling, and even morality are rooted there. Certain parts control different functions of reality, and when the chemicals change, a new cocktail of hormones flows into our bodies and our moods shift. For example, some women undergoing hormone replacement therapy report the loss of spiritual feelings or connectedness or the rise of an insipid form of skepticism about everything. Is this all just a matter of some neurological foundation?

As I have noted elsewhere, there's some evidence that suggests we can stimulate an area of the brain with an electrical signal and the subject will have a deep religious experience.[2] (This is somewhat controversial, especially in light of the fact that a Swedish team of scientists failed to replicate the original reports made by Persinger.) In short, once again, there appears to be a biological source for our every experience.

Knowing that can make it easier to sort out the false self from the authentic. For example, if I'm unaware of the predispositions that are simply a matter of being a human animal, I might be inclined to interpret information in a manner totally false to the real world but in keeping with my beliefs. The chemical cocktail that suggests a dreary day will influence how I take the comments made to me by others. On the other hand, give me a different mixture, one that fills me with exuberance, and I'll behave differently, to say nothing of react to others in a different fashion. Drug me, thereby inhibiting the amygdala, and I might charge a machine-gun bunker without fear of any kind. Using a different pharmaceutical can potentially arrest my inhibitions, turning me into an amoral animal.

The Authentic Self

If we assume that the environment combines with our hardwiring to deliver our choices and options, it's easy to see that finding the authentic self and nurturing it is much more difficult than adopting the false self so easily imitated from the world we inhabit. In our culture full of simulation, video games, movies, television, and the Internet, how do we preserve our true being?

First, of course, we must become fully educated—realize that others are trying to manipulate our choices and go out of our way to discover why. By exploring both sides of the equation, we'll be in a much better position to have our own opinions rather than taking on someone else's. In the process, we'll also be able to identify those practices and dissonant ideas that are causing our psyche stress and resulting in falsophrenic activities.

But I believe the best way to escape falsophrenia is through service. Our brains are also hardwired to reward us when we do things for others. As mentioned earlier, research has shown us that simply making a charitable donation causes the brain to release the body's natural opiates, endorphins. When I recognize that I'm physically designed for certain things, then I can choose behavior that leads to the greatest sense of self-actualization. For example, simply smiling causes the brain to release endorphins. We can therefore optimize our lives by being aware of our mind and body and the interface between them.

Reflection

The world we live in today is full of information, packed with stimuli, and often aimed at owning some of our thoughts. Our brains are wired in such a way as to exert direct influence over our emotions and consequently influence our thoughts and behavior. Knowing this can aid in preventing the loss of our true self, but being committed to service is our best way to avoid falsophrenia.

Why do you think service to others offers protection from falsophrenia—or do you?

CHAPTER 22

PEACE

"The poor long for riches, the rich long for heaven,
but the wise long for a state of tranquility."

— SWAMI RAMA

I believe in inner peace, and I believe in world peace. The first is easier to obtain than the latter, if for no other reason than it involves only one person to be successful. That is, we can choose peace on our own and with a few modifications obtain it—at least for a while. Perhaps I should say that we can *find* it, for I'm also convinced that once we have our place of calm, something will disturb it, showing us that we're not quite ready to walk on water. In other words, until and unless we gain perfection, we'll know periods when we must work to regain our sense of peace, and this is a never-ending cycle that continues until nothing can disturb us.

Inner peace is something we can achieve by practicing the principles of character that I've already discussed. Service, integrity, love, balance, and the like will all place us in a state of mind that allows tranquility to bathe our being. As Dale Carnegie put it, "If half a century of living has taught me anything at all, it has taught me that nothing can bring you peace but yourself." How about world peace, then—is that something we can truly believe in? I mean, is it really attainable?

How do we go about contributing to greater harmony? Let's assume for the moment that beginning right now, one of our daily priorities is to do something that contributes to world peace. What would that be? Would we argue the superiority of our forces, our philosophy, our way of government, our legal system, or just what? How would we reach out to those who find our way of life an abomination?

Disputes

What causes disputes between and within nations? Is it poverty, ideology, overcrowding, technology, or all of them and more? Perhaps we think that if we determine the root of the problem, we'll solve it. Maybe we should begin our commitment by working out the various areas that give rise to the differences that lead to wars, ethnic cleansing, and civil rioting. The problem is that when we look at the whole picture, we'll also find people rioting because their workweek or retirement age has been extended. Other violence is all about the world banking system or historical issues and the local enculturation. Many of the problems in certain areas of the Middle East are due to conflicts that have their roots in events that are hundreds of years old. And this says nothing about tyrannical despots ruling from their own agendas or religious zealots out to convert or kill the infidels. How, then, do we individually contribute daily to world peace?

There are many people who believe that everything is an illusion and that we are all one, and so, all we need do is send loving energy to those regions of the world and the violence will end. Maybe by our becoming the example, those despots who wish to keep all the power and prosperity for themselves will be shamed into relinquishing control. Now there are instances where this has worked, such as when Ashley Smith read excerpts of *The Purpose Driven Life* to an escaped killer, and as a result, he released her and turned himself in.[1] But this kind of stories isn't the norm. And while it may be okay to turn the other cheek when you've been wronged, is it really okay to do this when entire groups are being wronged? How about the women in the Congo or in Iran?

Be Informed and Act

I believe peace is accomplished through a multifaceted approach. First, we must become informed about the world we live in. We can't pretend worldly matters don't exist by shutting them out and remaining in our own little private realms. Oh, we may never know about many tragedies in the world by remaining reclusive, but I suggest that this response is denial and not spiritual enlightenment.

Assume we become informed; then we must do our part, either in the political process, if only by voting, or through the charitable organizations to which we choose to contribute. In other words, we must become both accountable and responsible for our efforts at increasing peace and understanding. That may mean we're donating time as well as money. Each of us must choose areas of the world to work on for peace, so if Ethiopia is your choice, then the contribution should be toward wiping out starvation and disease while building a stable and just civic administration.

We tend to let our government and other agencies worry about matters of this nature, and therefore we take no role in owning some part of the problem. As Immanuel Kant said, by doing this we fail to be intelligent—we let others make our decisions and thus stop thinking for ourselves.

I've written much about the brainwashing that goes on in the world and the sound bites everyone passes around as though they were meaningful axioms describing some truth in the world, when most are only partially true—and then only within a specific context and always with a loaded agenda. Once again, however, it's appropriate to remind you that making your own informed decision and taking on some part of the problem is the best way for you to contribute to world peace.

Next, it's incumbent upon each of us to be the change we seek. Mahatma Gandhi said, "Be the change you want to see in the world." We should therefore invest enough time in ourselves to become authentic and to find tranquility. Coming from this position is the best way to broker peace. Right now Norway is ranked as the most peaceful country in the world, according to the Global Peace Index, and the Dalai Lama is considered by many to be the most peaceful person in the world. What do this person and this country do to promote harmony? That which creates serenity is what each of us wants to promote within ourselves and the world around us. Teaching from example is always the strongest way.

Universal Declaration of Human Rights

Finally, at least within the scope of this conversation, each of us must do more than become informed: We must turn our information into action. Talking about it, investigating it, and donating to supportive organizations is only one leg of the solution. I believe that peace is possible but only when the vast majority of people on this planet desire it. Ending violence should be number one on our agenda—as individuals and as a collective group. This goal will never be achieved until and unless there's some accord between those with differences. As I write this, the task seems almost impossible. Still, I believe that it *is* possible, and it begins by settling on certain human rights. That was once done following World War II, and nearly every nation in the world signed on to it—the UN General Assembly resolution 217 A (III) was adopted and proclaimed the Universal Declaration of Human Rights on December 10, 1948.

Perhaps one of the best ways any of us can work toward ending conflict is to examine and begin to share and remind everyone of this apparently little-known document. There are many organizations dedicated to world peace, and most have some type of emissary. I believe we're all capable of being peace ambassadors, and when we all accept that challenge, our dream will be just that much closer.

The Choice for Peace

There's a tale about peace that begins with a bedtime story:

A man sat down with his sons to read a bedtime story, but his oldest son interrupted with a question: "Dad, is there going to be a war? I saw on the news that Koloya had shelled its neighbor and sunk one of their ships, killing everyone on board. Does that mean war? 'Cause, Dad, don't they both have nuclear weapons?"

The man paused before answering. "Now, I don't want either of you lads to worry about war. There have been many wars throughout history and they have taught us the futility of combat. There are basically good people running the various governments of the world, and they're wise beyond what you might hear on the news. No one wants what our Defense Department calls 'MAD,' short for Mutually Assured Destruction. Perhaps this story will illustrate my point:

"Once upon a time, there were rival nations on a far-away planet. These countries spent much of their resources building armies and developing weapons. They'd done this for years, and each year it seemed that more and more of the budget went for defense spending, until one day there simply wasn't enough money to cover the bills. Every nation had dedicated so much to national security that many of their citizens went without vital services, including police, fire, and emergency medical technicians.

"Almost in unison, the citizens of the world began to voice their disapproval. They did this by electing new officials and by demonstrating in countries where elections weren't used to select the leaders. The protests were modeled after those that liberated India, led by Gandhi. The people said, 'Enough—we have had enough.'

"At first, not much changed, but the noise from the citizens worldwide became louder and louder; and then one day, with nations borrowing money from each other and printing more money to pay their loans, the whole financial world melted down. Nation after nation found itself unable to pay its debts without printing even more money, which devalued their currency further and fed inflation, until, as in Germany following World War I, it took almost a whole wheelbarrow of money to buy a loaf of bread.

"There were two ways to change the financial crisis, and one was war. Historically, that's what had often happened to pull sinking economies out of the hole. However, the people of the world knew of this historical trend, and they'd have none of it. Almost in chorus, the world's citizens organized and spoke in one very loud voice: 'It will not be war—it will be peace.' It was the people of every nation that demanded peace and simply insisted on no more expenditures on war.

"At first, the governments were suspicious of each other, and while they dramatically cut back the spending, they still watched other nations carefully. But as they saw other countries responding to popular demand and cutting back their spending, every administration invested more in its own populace. As a result, nations began to excel in education, public welfare, and infrastructure maintenance. The debt that every country had incurred was paid, and leaders began to share a larger picture: how to improve the lives of everyone on the planet.

"Well, the bottom line, boys, is this: the world changed because people like you decided to change it. Before then, most simply acquiesced to whatever their leaders thought was the right thing to do regarding security. You know, when you plan for conflict, you get it; but when you plan for peace, that becomes possible, too. It's a delicate balance, but it can be done, and I believe you two boys will have a part in doing it."

With that, the boys gave their dad a hug, pulled the covers up tight under their chins, and fell asleep, where they dreamed of their roles in securing world peace.

Reflection

There was a time in our history when areas of America could only imagine safety and peace. Today, we know that criminals exist, and they'd have us acting as vigilantes were it not for our legal system. I believe in the rule of law. The world may always have some rogue nation that behaves like a criminal, but when everyone decides to live by the rule of law and agrees on universal rights, as they once did in 1948, an end of conflict becomes possible. It's not likely to happen without every one of us pitching in, however. I believe in peace, and I believe in you. What do you believe?

Do you think peace is possible? What do you think you would have to do to personally contribute to a more harmonious world? What can you do today to begin the process? Do you believe it's possible to have peace on Earth without first having it within?

CHAPTER 23

THE VALUE OF
MORTALITY

*"To suspect your own mortality is to know
the beginning of terror; to learn irrefutably that
you are mortal is to know the end of terror."*

— FRANK HERBERT

A few years ago, I underwent an unexpected triple-bypass heart surgery. There were several subtle shifts that accompanied this event. It truly was life changing but in ways you might not expect. For example, today I find myself unable to hold back the tears while watching acts of courage, sacrifice, or deep personal love. *Why,* I wondered, *would this be so? Could it be that the heart—as myth and legend have it—is the seat of emotion?*

I began to share my experience with others who'd gone through major surgery. I discovered that they, too, were unable to restrain the tears. Some of the men I spoke to were rough-and-tough cowboy types, former football players, and truck drivers—you wouldn't expect any of them to be overly emotional. Why? What had happened? Could it be a byproduct of the anesthesia?

I did a little more research, and I found that many people were reporting a special new sensitivity, an empathy, following surgery. Some of the procedures weren't particularly major. Anesthesiologist Gareth S. Kantor, M.D., theorized on the Internet that it could be due to a repressed memory about the surgery itself. That's a guess, and he conceded that. Unfortunately, as Dr. Kantor was quick to point out, anesthesiologists typically don't see their patients in the days that follow surgery.

Although the reports are many, the answers are few, and none are definitive. I suppose it could be said that after general anesthesia, tearing up over things that formerly would never have produced a single tear could be due to some cognitive impairment—that is, brain damage. That's an interesting question for a neurologist; but from my perspective and the input of those I've spoken with, I believe it's really more a matter of feeling somehow more mortal.

More Mortal

More mortal—what does that mean? The great mind of Augustine of Hippo, or St. Augustine, thought of the world as the place we lived in when we looked outward. It's full of beauty and beautiful things. Nothing is bad, for according to Augustine, everything is made by God. In his book *Confessions,* Augustine paints an emotional and poignant picture of a life turned away from God and the eternal. In his view, it's easy to be seduced by the physical environment. The beauty of the world creates an appetite for pleasure that takes our hand when we're very young and leads us ever further away from ourselves. It is when we turn back inward, to the very core of our being, that we find the presence of the eternal—the kingdom within. The glory of the eternal is so much more than what surrounds us that once we experience it, we don't go back.

In my mind, the solemnity of major surgery reminds us that the mortal self is not all there is. Once we recognize this and fully appreciate its meaning, not unlike those who have near-death experiences, our lives change. The empathy arises particularly when we behold the glory of humanness around us, and that's why it doesn't take a sad movie to trigger the crying.

I first experienced this in a chick flick that I saw with my wife. It was an ordinary story of a relationship between two people who loved each other to the core. For various reasons, their relationship came close to ending—indeed, we thought it was over. Then through a few near-magical events, they were brought back together to live happily ever after. I've seen many such films with my wife because I love her, but I'd generally failed to appreciate them. Not this time—I wept during the happy ending. *What the hell is this?* I asked myself.

For years I practiced criminalistics, and my life was threatened more than once. For recreation, I trained horses, sometimes wild horses that had been rounded up by the Bureau of Land Management. As a boy, I was in more fights than I can remember. I don't cry—or didn't.

All for Love

A day or two later, my wife and I watched another movie, this time one of my liking—*Armageddon*. In the end, Bruce Willis puts his daughter's intended fiancé on the ship for home and takes his place—a place drawn by straws for the one who would remain on the asteroid, set the charge, explode it, and thereby save Earth.

Throughout the movie, the two men have been at each other, and Willis has promised his daughter that he'll come home. Tears come to my eyes as I write this, so obviously I cried then.

The glory of the human condition is beyond words. As a species we can be so cruel, so conniving, so filled with enmity—yet there's this other side. There's a part of us that reaches beyond the needs of the individual, that's willing to pay the highest price for the good of our fellow humans, that knows no sacrifice too great for those we love and cherish, that simply is proof in and of itself of the Higher Creator who endowed the species with the ultimate "good," or god, within. It's the portrayal of these qualities that evokes the tears.

Perhaps if our species knew no temporal limits, we'd fail to recognize the highest level that we're all wired to express, to share— to *be*. Maybe major surgery reminds us all that we could be out of here, figuratively speaking, in the next breath. We're eternal, not from our indulgences with the outer world but from who we truly are at our innermost level of being.

This is a reminder that opens us up to the real beauty of the world we live in and to the people we truly are. Our human potential is so incredible that without its glory, I wonder if we'd even need tears. It's for this reason that I believe in the value of mortality.

Reflection

What do you believe? Is it possible to have an awakening without going through some life-threatening experience? What if you were to take time to acknowledge those special events that make living spectacular—not the major events that affect all of humankind but rather those small situations that occur every day. Do you believe this kind of thinking can add new depth and wonder to your journey?

CHAPTER 24

RELATIONSHIPS

"Shared joy is a double joy, shared sorrow is half a sorrow."
— SWEDISH PROVERB

The role belief plays in relationships can't be understated. However, while we may understand this role when it comes to our personal bonds, most of us do not realize that it also relates to other kinds of interactions as well. Did you know that studies now show that a leader's beliefs about his followers affects a company's success? Indeed, according to *Science Daily:* "How leaders view their employees tends to become a self-fulfilling prophecy, which affects company success. Managers' conceptions of employees affect job satisfaction, relationships and trust."[1]

Let's look at this diverse area of research for a moment and then turn our attention to those most personal and intimate dealings between significant others. One of the best-known and most prominent factors that has been researched is known as the *Pygmalion effect*. This phenomenon was first empirically demonstrated with teachers and their students. The design was simple: Inform the teachers that they were going to have a gifted child in class, and then give them a learning-challenged youngster and see what happens. By the end of the year, the children labeled as gifted had made dramatic gains in their learning ability and levels.[2] Obviously, the expectation factor is very important when we examine relationships.

This same factor may account for the interplay of expectations in the workplace, as well as in just about any other environment you can imagine. For example, the role authority plays today can be unnerving. The Pygmalion effect would suggest that our expectation of greater knowledge, experience, or power might just be why certain areas of our brain actually "turn off" in the presence of an authority, be it a physician, member of the clergy, or anyone in between. We can easily extrapolate that this authority issue covers the engagement between parents and children. Indeed, a fair question might be, *Under what circumstances does the role of a dominant member of a group, older sibling, or strong paternal leader fail to lead to arresting certain critical discernment abilities in the brains of the other members of the group?*

When we examine some of the classic experiments in psychology, ranging from the Stanford Prison Experiment to Stanley Milgram's infamous authority study—in which subjects continued to deliver to students what they thought were lethal shocks, based solely on the urging of the authority in the white coat—we find a human weakness or potential for evil. This is what Philip Zimbardo has dubbed the *Lucifer effect*.[3]

Herd Animals

Human beings are basically herd animals. Arguably, this is exactly why we seem to be hardwired to surrender power to a so-called higher authority. It's our herd instinct that gives rise to our socialization, and this process further galvanizes the need to be able to be a good follower. Our propensity for following then becomes another important element to understand in all interactions.

Thus, here are two important aspects to get our heads and hearts around with respect to relationships. There are more, of course, but our focus is on these two and the belief system that supports them. The first is our role as followers, and the second is the expectation factor.

But before continuing this investigation, we should examine disappointment. For example, what happens when our child refuses to follow our admonitions? The failure to follow can lead to serious breaches in relationships, just as going along with orders can lead to serious abuses. The role of expectation under both of these circumstances becomes critical, and that will always boil down to the belief system of the individual. Ideas about what's right and wrong are built on belief—they aren't written in stone so that everyone recognizes the authority. And alas, this in itself can contribute to problems in all relationships.

Friendship is an important part of our lives. Research continues to show the primacy of close ties and social activity in staying healthy and active. A recent study found that there are cultural differences to these roles and expectations:

> Chinese participants emphasized the moral quality of close friendship and the connection of friendship and society more than Western participants did and were more altruistic towards the third person. Western participants focused predominantly on interaction qualities and promise-keeping and, in particular, in late adolescence on relationship intimacy.[4]

Think of any relationship you have or desire. What is it you want from that connection? Does the other person share the same expectation? Here's the critical factor—if your ideas differ substantially, it will be very difficult to have a successful relationship. Just as with the difference between Chinese and Western cultures, if the expectations actually violate one another in certain areas, a genuine bond is not possible.

As herd animals, we may be easy followers, but within all of us is a need or desire to sometimes lead. This urge can also become a problem unless restricted to situations in which your guidance is accepted. Our ideas regarding matters of leading and following are really the issue.

Underlying our expectation is our belief system. For example, if the ethical aspect of life is important, then relationships that share a moral basis are much more likely to thrive than those that don't. So with this little bit of introduction, let's turn back to the personal side.

Codependence

Among many people, there's a certain attitude of codependence. This is often expressed in terms of a bargain, a contract, or a sort of *quid pro quo*. That is, we think, *You should do this for me because I do this for you. If you loved me, you'd do x, y, and z.* The notion implies a duty. For example, parents often assume codependent roles and expect their children to nearly kneel and worship them because of parental sacrifices. Building relationships on such patterns will almost always lead to resentment and disappointment.

Examining our motives is important. Where our closest, most intimate bonds are concerned, maintaining a realistic outlook is key. There will be many changes during a long-term personal relationship. The initial romance will wear off, the hormones will cool down, and the Cinderella nature of perfect love will curl up in a mature bonding, provided the connection isn't built on false assumptions and immature, unrealistic notions taken from movies and television shows.

It's estimated that approximately half the marriages in America will end in divorce. Further, this figure applies to first marriages versus later unions, since "67% of second and 74% of third marriages end in divorce, according to Jennifer Baker of the Forest Institute of Professional Psychology."[5]

There are many reasons for the high divorce rate, including disappointment, selfishness, demanding too much, economic differences, pettiness, blaming, laziness, and differences in values or faith. Inherent in all of these factors are the underlying beliefs each partner brings to the marriage. Surprising to many is that the lowest proportion of divorce belongs to atheists and agnostics. Perhaps that is because the initial expectation is simply more pragmatic. For the atheist, the connection is all about here and now; for the religious person, there are both explicit and implicit assumptions about unions made in heaven.

The actual reasons for divorce are not my point here, however. This book is all about the role of belief in our lives. It's easy to see that an unreasonable expectation will lead to a failed relationship. It's equally obvious that our expectations are built upon our beliefs, and if we're to enjoy our lives to the fullest, choosing what we believe and how and who we share those beliefs with is pivotal.

If you're having difficulties with someone, take a look at your assumptions and then consciously choose your course of action. That said, never be afraid to let someone go if that's what he or she wants. There's an old saying that goes like this: "If you love someone, let them go. If they come back, they were always yours; and if they don't, then they never were."

Reflection

What do you see in your relationships? Are your expectations blinding you to the real attributes of the other person? Are you denying yourself in your attempt to be what someone else would like you to be? These questions are really two sides of the same coin, but they're vital components to creating the kind of connection you want.

CHAPTER 25

THE MIND-BODY BELIEF SYSTEM

"The power of love to change bodies is legendary,
built into folklore, common sense, and everyday
experience. Love moves the flesh, it pushes matter around.
. . . Throughout history, 'tender loving care' has uniformly
been recognized as a valuable element in healing."

— LARRY DOSSEY

What we believe directly affects our health, and not just as a result of some peripheral matter such as ignoring the warnings about smoking and choosing to believe in the law of psychological exception—that is, "It couldn't happen to me." No, studies repeatedly show that the mind has the power not only to immunize us against disease but also to create illness.

This isn't news to some individuals, but most people conceive of this as a disorder in thinking—a psychosomatic matter or psychological condition known as *hypochondria*. The general public tends to view this as "imagining illness" or being so fearful of disease that patients mimic symptoms and therefore they're sick. The fact is, however, that the power of suggestion can actually create disease.

Hypnosis is a powerful tool when it comes to investigating the strength of the mind and its interaction with the body. Research has demonstrated repeatedly that subjects can be hypnotized, and then the suggestion that the hypnotist is burning them while touching them with an ice cube can lead to a physical blister identical to that produced by a burn. In fact, as I mentioned earlier, at least one scientific research committee, led by none other than Benjamin Franklin, found that hypnosis could regularly produce levitation—the mind making matter lighter than air and defying gravity. That group took great precautions to guard against faking, carefully checking for concealed trickery, and they still observed the phenomena enough to conclude that it demonstrated a true instance of floating in the air. In other words, levitation was at one time a yardstick proving the legitimacy of hypnosis.[1]

Placebos

Research with placebos—nontherapeutic substances that are commonly thought of as sugar pills—is also telling when it comes to the role of belief and the function of the mind in matters of wellness. When the faith and expectation of a subject invests in the power of the placebo, amazing things happen. What's more, the treatment is relative to the condition, so one false pill can treat pain half as well as aspirin *and* half as well as morphine. Not surprisingly, telling the patient that the same tablet increases discomfort will result in just that.

Placebos don't have to be pills; they can be creams, injections, or even surgery. Just as interesting, the effect is larger if you increase the dosage size—say a larger capsule or two of them. Further, research shows that a branded item works better than a plain one, one in a shiny box elicits greater results than one in a plain package, a capsule trumps a tablet, with an injection working even better. If you use fancy, expensive-looking, sophisticated equipment, it yields even more dramatic outcomes. The bottom line is that the greater the expectation, the greater the effect. In other words, building a strong belief creates the foundation for the result.[2]

There are still more revealing facts about placebos that dovetail directly into our human psychology. For example, color is often employed to evaluate mood states, as in the Lüscher Color Test. The validity of this test has been determined to be overall 81 percent in agreement with the Taylor-Johnson Temperament Analysis.[3] So how does color correlate with the placebo effect? Well, blue is more effective as a "downer," and red is the preferred color for an "upper." Further, as Daniel Keogh and Luke Harris point out in their very informative Internet film, studies have shown that people who take their medication on a regular basis are much less likely to die than those who don't adhere to their drug regimen, even if they're only taking placebos. If that's not enough to convince you of the power of belief, then try this one. Again, the creators of the aforementioned film point out that placebos can also be addictive. In one study, 40 percent of the women who'd taken an inactive medication for five years suffered withdrawal symptoms.[4]

Remember that by definition, there's no medical value to a placebo. It's not what's in the substance that matters but what we put in it via our belief. Clever researchers can weight our belief by feeding an already expectant psychology with the right color, shape, size, and so forth to further ensure the maximum effect![5]

That's right, a genuine medical result from a nonmedical intervention. It's clearly our minds that have the power.

Mass Hysteria

Another area of research that continues to amaze many is known as *mass hysterical illness*. This phenomenon is also known as *group hysteria, collective hysteria,* and *mass psychogenic illness.* Typically, one individual will report symptoms that others then begin to manifest.

Take, for instance, this account of a Malaysian school in 2001:

> More than 30 secondary school girls were struck Monday by an unexplained hysteria for almost four hours during a routine morning assembly in a Malaysian school, the Sun reported Tuesday. Some 1,100 students, both boys and girls, at Puchong Perdana National School in the outskirts of Kuala Lumpur had gathered in the school field for a weekly Monday assembly at 7.30 A.M. when suddenly a 15-year-old girl started screaming, then collapsed.
>
> This led to a chain reaction. The rest of the students ran to their classrooms in panic when at least 30 girls began acting violently, throwing objects and screaming. The school headmaster, Aris Ahmad, teachers and state education department officers took four hours to calm down the affected girls.
>
> Both the affected and unaffected students are being given counseling. One of the victims, Nor Hasni Hassan, 16, told the Sun, "I only remember staggering for a distance after hearing the screams of my schoolmates before collapsing."[6]

Or consider this story from Mexico in 2007:

> The teenage girls hobbled into a prayer meeting at their Catholic boarding school, their knees buckling with every step. For months, a mysterious illness had swept through their school, afflicting hundreds of girls, and they were there to ask for recovery.

The first isolated cases of the illness, which affected the girls' walking and made them feverish and nauseated, appeared in November and December. After the girls came back from Christmas break, the illness spread. By February, the school's director, Sister Margie Cheong, had become alarmed and alerted the authorities.

At the Wednesday prayer meeting, Sister Michaela Shim handed out cookies and began to tell a story in her Korean-accented Spanish. The girls laughed and shouted as her improvised parable unfolded. It was the story of a boy who lies to get attention.

What may be happening here is far more complex. After batteries of tests, doctors now believe that the illness that has struck 600 of the 3,600 girls at this charity-run school is psychological.

In medical terms, Mexico's public health authorities have concluded that the girls at the Children's Village School are suffering from a mass psychogenic disorder. In layman's language, they have a collective hysteria. It is a diagnosis that doctors are usually hesitant to make, concerned that they might miss any other cause, and uncomfortable with nineteenth-century images of screaming girls, trances or collective delusions.

But Victor Manuel Torres Meza, director of epidemiology for the Mexico State health department, said there were about 80 documented cases from around the world. They are usually in closed communities, like schools and factories, and they tend to occur more frequently among adolescents and among girls.[7]

In short, the power of your belief is absolutely enormous and has long-standing consequences for your health and wellness.

One area that's gaining attention is aging. Think right now about how you expect a 90-year-old to look. Think about an 80-year-old or someone who's 70 or 60, and you begin to see that you have preconceptions regarding the aging process. What's known is this: If you expect that a 70-year-old will be feeble and use a cane, that's likely what you'll get.

I remember seeing a program as the year 2000 approached. This film featured people who were alive when the year 1900 arrived, and of course many were more than 100 years old. What

amazed me was the difference between what I'd expected someone of that age to look and be like and what the filmmakers
showed. For the most part, many of these centenarians looked as
though they were in their 60s and early 70s. They were fit, agile,
and alert in every way. Some did daily workouts that would put
many in their 40s to shame. It became clear to me at that moment:
If I wanted to remain fit and healthy into my 90s and later, I was
going to have to change my mental image of what someone that
age would be like in every way.

The film was a great wake-up call to me and is still a model
upon which I base my ideas about aging. What's your expectation?

Expecting to Die

Years ago, I did some research regarding the role of the mind
in wellness, and it eventually led to a CD training collection and
companion book, *Wellness: Just a State of Mind?* One of the studies I
came across was most interesting and relevant to the whole matter
of my beliefs regarding aging and, for that matter, dying. In this
case, the Chinese birth sign was used to compare death with the
expectation factor. According to the Chinese system of astrology,
each birth sign provides information about individuals in terms
of their occupational proclivities, talents, interests, and even the
eventual cause of death. According to researcher David Phillips,
the data showed a clear relationship between the astrological sign
and the cause of death. In other words, if because of astrology you
believed you'd die of cancer, then cancer is what you got.[8]

The Health Belief Model (HBM) has been evaluated in a number of studies since the early 1970s when this whole model of psy-
choneuroimmunology (now known as PNI) began to gain some
real traction among health-care professionals. One of the most
significant factors to emerge from the research is the influence of
what are referred to as "perceived barriers."[9]

The Authority Figure

Several years ago, I conducted research that involved patients diagnosed with cancer. I used a cognitive approach by employing an audio recording (my InnerTalk technology) designed to fundamentally influence what the subjects thought to be true, generating a positive outlook and confidence in the body's ability to heal itself. In other words, the design of the study sought to measure the influence of a change in beliefs on the progression of cancer.

In short, this is what we found: First, every single patient who believed that the mind had a role in wellness, and whose physician believed this as well, was in complete remission (no evidence of cancer). By contrast, every single individual whose doctor reported that the mind had no role in wellness was dead. In a sense, it didn't matter what the patient thought within this latter group—it all depended upon the medical authority.

Even though this was just a small test group, the results disturbed and puzzled me. That puzzlement changed recently when science learned through the use of functional magnetic resonance imaging (fMRI) that "parts of the prefrontal and anterior cingulate cortices, which play key roles in vigilance and skepticism when judging the truth and importance of what people say, were deactivated" in the presence of an authority. While the first study I noticed of this nature was about the clergy, other studies show that this effect includes anyone we think of as an authority.[10]

Similar to the power of the placebo, it appears that the healthcare professional can reverse the positive by informing us that matters are out of our hands, and as with the cancer patients in the study, we'll just surrender to their preconceptions and die.

Psychologist Ernest Rossi has argued for years that the mind can and does actually change the DNA molecule. His pioneering work in this area has been aimed at bringing the healing arts into the world of neurogenesis. He explains:

> We've discovered what the mind-body connection is really all about. This comes from the middle 1990s—neuroscience found that experiences of novelty, enrichment, exercise, both

mental and physical, turn on activity-dependent gene expression, and that turns on brain plasticity, modulates the immune system, and activates stem cells throughout the body. And we've just completed a study, published last year for the first time— we used DNA microarrays to evaluate therapeutic hypnosis in psychotherapy. For the first time, we've established that therapeutic hypnosis in psychotherapy does change gene expression— specifically activity-dependent or experience-dependent gene expression.[11]

Reflection

It now seems obvious: What we believe predisposes our expectation and behavior. It directly influences our health, sense of well-being, and even the aging process. So what is it that you anticipate? Do you think you'll "catch" the cold, flu, or other "bug" that's going around? Do you assume you'll be sick for a certain amount of time? Does it seem that some illnesses are more likely at a specific age, under certain conditions, or simply because of genetics? What would happen if you changed your own beliefs about this? Is it possible that you could become healthier, avoid many of the infections that go around, and recover more quickly when you do become sick? Many people are reporting just this result.

Again, we find just how incredibly important it is to choose carefully what we believe.

CHAPTER 26

I BELIEVE IN YOU

*"Do not believe in anything simply because
you have heard it. Do not believe in anything simply
because it is spoken and rumored by many. Do not believe in
anything simply because it is found written in your religious
books. Do not believe in anything merely on the authority
of your teachers and elders. Do not believe in traditions
because they have been handed down for many generations.
But after observation and analysis, when you find that
anything agrees with reason and is conducive to the good
and benefit of one and all, then accept it and live up to it."*

— BUDDHA

Benjamin Franklin is reported to have said, "Believe half of what you see and none of what you hear." I believe it's wise to question the information fed to us, especially in our day of media-ocracy.

I can say unequivocally that I believe in human potential. I've been blessed to work with a variety of individuals in all walks of life from elite athletes and successful entrepreneurs to addicts and criminals. I've dedicated much of my life to developing technologies that assist people in changing deep-seated, self-destructive patterns; and I guarantee you, tigers can change their stripes.

A couple of years ago, I met up with my associate and colleague from Germany, Antony Fedrigotti. We try to get together every couple of years, and when we do, we meet in Las Vegas—where else? We often enter the MGM Grand casino's buffet early for a brunch and end up talking for hours. The last time we did so, we were both troubled by world affairs. Antony teaches essentially the same thing I do, and he represents my InnerTalk technology exclusively where the German language is concerned. We've been friends and business associates for more than 20 years.

I Believe

Antony and I talked about what might be done about the violence and hate in the world and finally decided that it would begin with the individual. Both of us committed to do our best to facilitate that. We also brainstormed an approach that would employ the InnerTalk technology to assist in making a change from the inside out for all who listened.

Conflict is possible only when you have a "them" and an "us," and the early stages of wars can often be found in these kinds of separations. We thought that our best contribution to world peace would be in our creation of an InnerTalk program that would wipe out the ideas of difference and focus on the joys of being human. I postulated that true harmony, both internal and external, could be created this way.

To that end, we created the program titled *I Believe*. The affirmations for it are in the Appendix, and they're all about recognizing and fully appreciating the similarities between all the people of the world. The script begins this way: *I believe in peace. I believe in the sacredness of life. I believe that all life is sacred. I believe there is a future for our children. I believe in caring for our planet. I believe in caring for others.* Well, I'm sure you get the gist.

Can it really be this simple? I truthfully don't know. Antony and I decided to create the program in as many languages as we could, and we've followed through on that resolution. We agreed to make it available free, and your copy came with this book. (You may also view the short video of this program by going to **http://www.eldontaylor.com/I_Believe**.) I'll master the program in more languages if native speakers step up and record the affirmations. But even then, can global peace really be accomplished by transforming one person at a time?

Yin and Yang

I think so—it is that simple. I believe that people inherently have within them both the yin and the yang of the outside world. Research clearly shows that lying dormant in the average person is the ability to do absolutely cruel things. Studies modeled on the book *Lord of the Flies* show that's exactly how we behave. The now-infamous Stanford experiment could have been used to predict perfectly the reprehensible events that transpired at Abu Ghraib. Other experiments and incidents such as this include the previously mentioned Stanley Milgram authority experiment; the Genovese, or bystander, effect, which indicates that the average honest person won't get involved while heinous crimes are committed; and more. [1, 2] The list is frighteningly long to someone who believes in the human potential as I do. That said, there's a side of humanity that inspires even the most pessimistic among us.

There are many stories of apparently reprehensible people who do truly great things, and movies are full of villains who reverse their roles and turn good, because that's a story line everyone loves. We all love redemption! In fact, many of us would like to be the catalyst that turns the bad to good, which is part of the reason so many women are attracted to so-called bad boys.

We also cherish our heroes—as we should—and many of us dream about fulfilling that role for someone some day. Stories of these exceptional people inspire us to reach for greatness. Sacrifice is what often makes heroes.

The Divinity Within

I believe that within the human potential rests Divinity, and I do mean something related to God. You're a miracle, and a spark of the Creator exists inside you. Indeed, I think that when Jesus said, "You will do all that I can do and more," and, "Why would you use my words and not do my deeds," that he meant these things literally. "My Father has many mansions," is another statement attributed to Christ, and when you review it, you must also remember the passage: "The kingdom of heaven is within." Your mansion, your kingdom is internal, and so is the Christ consciousness. "If you but have faith the size of a mustard seed," you can move mountains. All of this I believe exists within you and every other human being.

What, then, does it take to manifest that inner glory? Everywhere you look, there's someone or something—text, mantra, or mandala—that allegedly will jump-start your progress or is the true path, yet I still know no one who walks on water. Why is that?

I believe that only you can "do the doing." Only you can breathe for you. I'm reminded of a wonderful story told by Hermann Hesse in his marvelous, must-read book, *Siddhartha*. He tells of a young man (the title character) who, through many trials, learns the ways of the sacred teachers, only to find that they aren't enlightened. When he finally meets the Buddha, he recognizes that having an enlightened teacher doesn't mean that you'll reach that state yourself. It's clear to Siddhartha that just as with doing your own breathing, you must do what's necessary yourself, and no amount of information or teaching can accomplish it for you. Realizing this, the young man eventually discovers himself after dealing with a number of hardships. A simple routine of daily work in the ebb and flow of the great river of life brings Siddhartha peace. I'm inclined to think of this as "living into yourself."

Losing Ourselves

In our modern society, we tend to lose ourselves in a number of ways. As young people, we practice matching an image, usually one out of the movies. The character we choose may be an amalgamation, but we all search for an identity that will bring us maximum pleasure and minimum pain. We also have psychological mechanisms such as compensation that come along and adjust our self-image. Thus a physically small person may emphasize intellectual pursuits and abilities, sparring with knowledge and vocabulary; a rich person may use wealth for power, while someone else employs physical force or athletic ability. In this way, we carve out who we think we are, but it's never our true self.

Next, we buy hook, line, and sinker the notion that we should look a certain way, and off we go, doing our best to meet that new image. As we age, we do everything we can to look younger than we are. In this way, we continue to hold self-discovery in abeyance. Some will never "live into" their authentic being for these reasons. This group includes those who insist that the real self isn't connected with what they look like, while they have face-lifts, use hair color, have Botox treatments, and more. If that's the case, why do these folks put so much money and effort into them in the first place?

Live into Yourself

I've been asked, "What does 'live into it' mean?" Think of it this way: you're living a journey through the world. Sooner or later, you'll arrive at a tomorrow that holds something that can't be known today. You'll just have to wait and live into that moment in order to meet your destiny. It's simple enough. You'll find that much of your life's meaning—and specifically the answers to such heavy questions as *Who am I?* and *Why here and now?*—must be lived into in order to be known.

We all lie to ourselves about many things. We can continually tell ourselves only what we want to hear. Author Chris Carter shared a metaphor with me that I like. He says that many of us hold beliefs as if they were our possessions, and woe betide anyone who tries to shatter them. Among those precious concepts are the ones we have about ourselves.

Highest Self

I believe that every human being has the ability to realize the highest self; indeed, we're continually nudged to evaluate our lives and thereby discover our real self, which is the only pathway up. Perhaps I should amend my statement to say, "every normal human being," because there are those who, due to some brain impairment or disorder, are sociopaths or behave like them. I believe that none of us will find what we seek in life until and unless we first find our authentic self. Once we find that, love and acceptance—indeed the nature of our true eternal being—becomes self-evident.

I believe that you're a miracle, and discovering your true self uncovers that wonder in a way that transcends the normal way of knowing. Like someone who undergoes a near-death experience and returns to this world, everything about your perspective can be changed. I don't believe you need to die to have this understanding, but the false self must be discarded and in some ways must perish for the authentic core to rise.

I believe the surest path to self-discovery comes through virtue. Being a good human is still a virtue. This means having a moral code and living up to it to the best of your ability. It's more than just high ideals; it's way of living, a code of conduct. This is the basis of character, which no one has at birth and which most people will have messed up in many ways before they realize its importance. That said, it's never too late to build character, and it's done just as you might construct a house, one brick at a time.

Reflection

I believe in you and your character, and I know that your example will profoundly affect many people. In that way, you can be an agent in creating a better way to live, a better world to live in, and a better way to know yourself.

How about you? Do you believe in yourself enough to know that your example does make a difference? Are you prepared today to start being the person you choose to be, to cultivate those character traits that will cause others to perceive you as being enlightened? What kind of difference would that make in your life?

EPILOGUE

"Mistakes are the inevitable accompaniment of the greatest gift given to man—individual freedom of action. . . . Let us be glad of the dignity of our privilege to make mistakes, glad of the wisdom that enables us to recognize them, glad of the power that permits us to turn their light as a glowing illumination along the pathway of our future. Mistakes are the growing pains of wisdom. Without them there would be no individual growth, no progress, no conquest."

— WILLIAM GEORGE JORDAN

We've all made mistakes, but they're no more than a low score on a life lesson. We all get tests every day, and they give us the opportunity to improve our score, eventually not just passing but excelling at the examination. All of this is a given ability once we recognize it as such.

There's no power on earth as powerful as you are. It's often said that love is the strongest force, but that emotion requires an object. Within you is a vast, largely untapped reservoir of energy that will manifest just as quickly as you learn to believe in yourself.

Love has accounted for remarkable deeds. It has healed the dying, saved the imperiled, warmed the heart in ways that words fail to express adequately, inspired nations, raised the consciousness of the world, and so much more. Drawing on this power, manifesting it, begins by caring for something more than you care for yourself. The authentic self knows this truth.

I believe that one of the most frequently asked questions about life comes down to *What's my path?* The answer is written in the hearts and minds of all humanity, and it amounts to no more and no less than service. Unconditional love manifests easily when we genuinely work for the benefit of another.

This book is about what to believe, and it has been my honor and pleasure to share my thinking on life's meaning—on the path and on all of those "I believe" moments—with you. Whatever else you take away, I hope you gain love for yourself, an awe for life, the recognition that character charters self-discovery, and the knowledge that service defines the self-actualized—for service is the doorway leading to our authentic selves.

Thank you for the read,

Eldon

APPENDIX

I Believe

I believe in peace.
I believe in the sacredness of life.
I believe that all life is sacred.
I believe there is a future for our children.
I believe in caring for our planet.
I believe in caring for others.
I believe in promoting peace, balance, and harmony.
I accept peace for myself.
I accept balance and harmony.
I am calm and peaceful.
I am rational and peace oriented.
I love life.
I believe life loves me.
I love living.
I enjoy every moment.
I treasure the experience of peace.
I act peacefully.
I think of peaceful solutions.
I seek peace in all my dealings.
I am loving.
I am caring.
I am sharing.
I am helpful.
I am healthy.
I am happy.

I BELIEVE

I choose wise choices.
I choose peaceful choices.
I choose helpful choices.
I am grateful.
I have a gratitude attitude.
I find good in all.
I celebrate life with every breath.
I find joy in life.
I still sense awe in the majesty of life.
I share my love for peace.
I believe in the rule of law.
I envision a peaceful world.
I hold the vision in my mind of a world at peace.
I believe we are all connected.
I believe in supporting others.
I find ways to help others.
I love helping other people.
I enjoy service.
I like it when others feel good.
My life has purpose.
Helping is part of my purpose.
Aiding others is rewarding.
I believe in family.
I believe the world is my extended family.
I meet each day with gratitude and joy.
Today I make a difference in the world.
Today I add peace to the world.
Everyday, in every way, we all improve.
I am an optimist.
My thoughts are powerful.
My thoughts create.
My creative force joins with all to create peace.
My creative force is behind world peace.
Thank you,
Thank you,
Thank you.

Appendix

I forgive myself.
I forgive all others.
I am forgiven.

This program also includes the symbiotic messages as published in Eldon's book *Subliminal Learning.*

ENDNOTES

Chapter 1

1. Mandino, O. 1990. *A Better Way to Live.* New York, NY: Bantam Books.

2. Glen Rein, G., and Rollin McCraty, R. 1993. "Local and non-local effects of coherent heart frequencies: On conformational changes of DNA." *Proceedings of the Joint USPA/IAPR Psychotronics Conference,* Milwaukee, WI.

3. Glanville, J. 1680. *Saducismus Triumphatus.* London: Printed by T. Newcomb, for S. Lownds, 1682. In Annenberg Rare Book and Manuscript Library. BF1581 .A2 1682. **http://sceti.library .upenn.edu/sceti/printedbooksNew/index.cfm?TextID =glanvill_1&PagePosition=3** and **http://www.thelivingmoon .com/44cosmic_wisdom/02files/Levitation05.html.**

4. Wikipedia. 2010. "Mystical Levitation in Christianity." **http://en.wikipedia.org/wiki/Levitation _(paranormal)#Mystical_levitation_in_Christianity.**

5. Niemi, M. B. 2009. "Placebo Effect: A Cure in the Mind." *Scientific American.* February 25, 2009.

6. Ibid.

7. Karam, E. G., and Khattar, L. H. 2007. "Mass psychogenic illness (epidemic sociogenic attacks) in a village in Lebanon." *J Med Liban.* 2007 Apr–Jun; 55(2):112-5.

8. Talbot, M. 1991. *The Holographic Universe.* New York, NY: Harper Perennial.

9. Radin, D. 2006. *Entangled Minds.* New York, NY: Pocket Paraview.

10. **http://www.princeton.edu/pear/**

11a. McTaggart, L. 2002. *The Field: The Quest for the Secret Force of the Universe.* New York, NY: HarperCollins.

11b. Targ, R. 2005. *Mind Reach: Scientists Look at Psychic Abilities.* Newburyport, MA: Hampton Roads Pub.

12. Massey, H. 2009. *Science of the Lost Symbol.* http://www .scienceofthelostsymbol.com/Human-Influence-on-Liv ing-and-Non-living-Systems.html.

13. Puthoff, H. E. 1996. "CIA-Initiated Remote Viewing at Stan ford Research Institute." *Journal of Scientific Exploration,* Vol. 10, No. 1, pp. 63–76

14. Backster, C. 2003. *Primary Perception: Biocommunication with Plants, Living Foods, and Human Cells.* Anza, CA: White Rose Millennium Press.

15. Puthoff, H. E., and Fontes, R. 1975. "Organic Biofield Sen sor." *Electronics and Bioengineering Laboratory Stanford Research Institute*–S.R.I Project 3194 (Task 3).

16. Lipton, B. 1991. Private communication.

17. Cromie, W. J. 2002. "Meditation changes tempera- tures: Mind controls body in extreme experiments." *Harvard University Gazette.* http://news.harvard.edu/ gazette/2002/04.18/09-tummo.html

18. Kurzweil, A. I. 2011. "Meditation May Change Brain's Physical Structure, Strengthen Connections." NHNE Pulse. http://nhne-pulse.org/medita tion-may-change-brains-physical-structure/?utm_ source=feedburner&utm_medium=email&utm_campaign =Feed%3A+nhnepulse+%28NHNE+Pulse%29

19 Romains, J. 1960. "CIA Study on Brainwashing." http:// www.fdrs.org/brainwashing_america.html

Chapter 3

1. U.S. Supreme Court. 1927. Buck v. Bell, 274 U. S. 200 (1927) http://supreme.justia.com/us/274/200/case.html

2a. Unknown. 2010. Pakistan: women unite to appeal for life of Christian condemned for blasphemy. Spero News. http:// www.speroforum.com/site/article.asp?idCategory=33&id sub=122&id=43436&t=Pakistan%3A+women+unite+to+a ppeal+for+life+of+Christian+condemned+for+blasphemy

2b. Wikipedia. 2011. Asia Bibi. http://en.wikipedia.org/wiki/ Asia_Bibi

2c. McCarthy, J. 2010. "Christian's Death Verdict Spurs Holy Row in Pakistan." NPR. December 14, 2010 . **http://www. npr.org/2010/12/14/132031645/christian-s-death-verdict-spurs-holy-row-in-pakistan**

Chapter 4

1. Mill, J. S. 1961. *Essential Works of J. S. M.: Utilitarianism Autobiography, On Liberty, The Utility of Religion.* Edited by Max Lerner. New York, NY: Bantam Books.

2. Kennedy, J. F. 1966. Day of Affirmation Address. **http ://www.jfklibrary.org/Research/Ready-Reference/RFK -Speeches/Day-of-Affirmation-Address-news-release-text -version.aspx**

3. Grube, G. M. A., trans., and Reeve, C. D. C. 1992. *Plato: Republic.* Cambridge, MA.: Hackett Publishing Co.

Chapter 6

1. Dürer, A. 1508. The Praying Hands. **http://en.wikipedia .org/wiki/File:Duerer-Prayer.jpg**

Chapter 7

1. **http://www.merriam-webster.com/dictionary/evil**

2. Freier, N. G. 2007. "Children Distinguish Conventional from Moral Violations in Interactions with a Personified Agent." *CHI 2007,* April 28–May 3, 2007, San Jose, CA. ACM 978-1-59593-642 4/07/0004. **http://vsdesign.org/publications/ pdf/p2195-freier.pdf**

3. Lewis, C. S. 2001. *Mere Christianity.* San Francisco, CA: HarperSanFrancisco

Chapter 8

1. Principe, L. M., ed. 2006. *Science and Religion.* Chantilly, VA: The Teaching Company.

2. Ibid.

3. Ibid.

4. Ibid.

5. Ibid.

6. Ibid.

7. Ibid.

8. Yudkowsky, E. S. 2008. "Mundane Magic." http://lesswrong.com/tag/naturalism/?sort=top

9. Wikipedia. 2011. "Demographics of Atheism." http://en.wikipedia.org/wiki/Demographics_of_atheism

10. Harris, S. 2006. "10 Myths—and 10 Truths—About Atheism." *Los Angeles Times* OpEd Page, Dec. 24, 2006. http://www.edge.org/3rd_culture/harris06/harris06_index.html

11. Dawkins, R. 2008. *The God Delusion.* Boston, MA: Mariner Books.

12. Anfinsen, as cited in Margenau and Varghese, "Cosmos, Bios, Theos," 1997. 139.

13. *Darwin Correspondence Project.* Letter 8837. http://www.darwinproject.ac.uk/entry-8837

14. Descartes, R. *The Meditations.* Trans. John Veitch 1901. Athenaeum Library of Philosophy. http://evans-experientialism.freewebspace.com/descartesmeditations01.htm

15. Taylor, E. 2009. *What Does That Mean?* Carlsbad, CA: Hay House.

16. Weaver, W. 1982. *Lady Luck: The Theory of Probability.* Mineola, NY: Dover Publications.

17. de Saint-Exupery, A. http://www.poemhunter.com/antoine-de-saint-exupery/quotations/

Chapter 9

1. Dalai Lama. http://thinkexist.com/quotation/as_human_beings_we_all_want_to_be_happy_and_free/145357.html

2. Kavanaugh, K., and Rodriguez, O. 1991. *The Collected Works of St. John of the Cross.* Washington, DC: ICS Publications.

3a. Minnigerode, L. 2005. Infants and Touch. **http://www .googobits.com/articles/2950-infants-and-touch.html**

3b. Harmon, K. 2010. "How Important Is Physical Contact with Your Infant?" *Scientific American,* May 6, 2010. **http://www .scientificamerican.com/article.cfm?id=infant-touch**

4. Woolf, V. 1929. A Room of One's Own. Boston, MA.: Mariner Books.

Chapter 11

1. Taylor, E. 1992. *Wellness: Just a State of Mind?* Medical Lake, WA: R. K. Books.

2. Taylor, E. 2007. *Choice and Illusions.* Carlsbad, CA: Hay House.

3. **http://thinkexist.com/quotation/what-do-you-first-do -when-you-learn-to-swim-you/367079.html**

Chapter 12

1. **http://thinkexist.com/quotation/if_we_study_the_lives _of_great_men_and_women/296966.html**

Chapter 13

1. **http://www.brainyquote.com/quotes/quotes/g /georgespa143694.html**

Chapter 14

1. Rosenthal, R., and Jacobson, L. 1992. Pygmalion in the Classroom. New York, NY: Irvington.

Chapter 15

1. Ritter, M. 2010. "Study: Vegetative Brains Show Signs of Awareness." Newsvine.com. **http://www.newsvine.com /_news/2010/02/03/3850507-study-vegetative-brains -show-signs-of-awareness**

Chapter 16

1. Osbon, D. K. 1995. *A Joseph Campbell Companion: Reflections on the Art of Living*. New York, NY: Harper Perennial.

Chapter 20

1. King, M. L., Jr. 1968. "The Drum Major Instinct." Delivered at Ebenezer Baptist Church, Atlanta, Georgia, February 4, 1968.

Chapter 21

1. Rohr, R. 2003. *Everything Belongs*. New York, NY: The Crossroad Publishing Company.
2a. Wikipedia 2010. Phineas Gage. **http://en.wikipedia.org/ wiki/Phineas_Gage**
2b. O'Driscoll, K. and Leach, J. P. 1998, "No longer Gage." *British Medical Journal*. December 19; 317(7174): 1673–1674. **http:// www.ncbi.nlm.nih.gov/pmc/articles/PMC1114479/**

Chapter 22

1. Noonan, P. 2005. "The Amazing Story of How Ashley Smith Stopped Brian Nichols's Killing Spree." *Wall Street Journal* Digital Network. March 18 2005 **http://online.wsj.com/ article/SB122470838006259761.html**

Endnotes

Chapter 24

1. Unknown. 2011. "Leader Beliefs about Followers Impact Company Success." University of California–Riverside, Science Daily. http://www.sciencedaily.com/releases/2011/04/110426091134.htm

2. Rosenthal, R., and Jacobson, L. 1992. *Pygmalion in the Classroom.* New York, NY: Irvington.

3. Zimbardo, P. 2007. *The Lucifer Effect.* New York, NY: Random House.

4. Keller, M. 2005. "A Cross-Cultural Perspective on Friendship Research." *ISBBD Newsletter.* Serial No. 46(2),10–11, 14.

5. http://www.divorcerate.org/

Chapter 25

1. Laurence, J., and Perry, C. 1988. *Hypnosis, Will, and Memory: A Psycho-Legal History.* New York, NY: The Guilford Press.

2. Keogh, D., and Harris, L. L. 2009. The Placebo Effect. http://nhne-pulse.org/video-the-placebo-effect/

3. Donnelly, F. A. 1977. "The Lüscher Color Test: A validity study." *Perceptual and Motor Skills* Vol 44(1)(Feb 1977): 17–18.

4. Keogh, D., and Harris, L. L. 2009. *The Placebo Effect.* http://nhne-pulse.org/video-the-placebo-effect/

5. Ibid.

6. Kyodo News International. 2001. *"Mass Hysteria hits Malaysian School."* http://findarticles.com/p/articles/mi_m0WDP/is_2001_July_16/ai_77057810/

7. Malkin, E. 2007. "At a School for the Poor, a Mysterious Illness." *New York Times,* April 16, 2007. http://www.nytimes.com/2007/04/16/world/americas/16mexico.html

8. Phillips, D. 1994. "Does Belief Influence the Outcome of Certain Diseases?" *The Lancet.* 342:1142–1145.

9. Janz, N. K., and Becker, M. 1984. "The Health Belief Model: A Decade Later." *Health Educ Behav.* March 1984, vol. 11, no. 1, 1–47 http://heb.sagepub.com/content/11/1/1.short

10. Schjoedt, U., et al. 2010. "The Power of Charisma—Perceived Charisma Inhibits the frontal executive network of believers in intercessory prayer." *Social Cognitive and Affective Neuroscience.* Doi:10.1093/scan/nsq023.

11. Aponte, R. 2009. "An Interview with Ernest Rossi, Ph.D." *Psychotherapy.net.* **http://www.psychotherapy.net /interview/ernest-rossi**

Chapter 26

1. Milgram, S. 1963. "Behavioral Study of Obedience." *Journal of Abnormal and Social Psychology.* 67, 371–378.

2. Wikipedia. "Murder of Kitty Genovese." **http://en .wikipedia.org/wiki/Kitty_Genovese**

ACKNOWLEDGMENTS

Acknowledging the importance of others is a necessary step in understanding the interdependent nature of life and its accomplishments.

I want first to acknowledge with special recognition my lovely wife, Ravinder, who works tirelessly, seeing to every minute detail in my manuscripts, especially that tedious task called a Bibliography. I also wish to recognize and express my appreciation to a new editor, Gyatri Devi, who made many contributions to this book. I also want to recognize the fine people at Hay House, who as a team make things easy for their authors in so many ways. It's both a pleasure and an honor to have Hay House as my publisher. That said, I must single out my Hay House editor Jessica Kelley, who also made many valuable contributions to this work. And to all at Hay House—my special thanks! I wish also to acknowledge my good friend and faithful editor of nearly 30 years, Suzanne Brady, who polishes my words as no one else can. Thank you Suzanne!

I've stated before that advancement comes only on the shoulders of many who have come before, marked out their specialty, delivered their epistles, spoken their soliloquies, written their classic works, debated their metaphysical foundations, philosophized about being and nothingness, sanitized their sciences, modeled their mathematics, and so much more. It goes without saying that to them—all of them—I owe a great debt, and this can't be overstated.

It's with deep humility that I continue to enjoy the great works of so many others while I strive to develop my own small contribution. This result would be nothing at all without the minds that went before me, including the One Mind behind it all.

ABOUT THE AUTHOR

Eldon Taylor is an award-winning, *New York Times* best-selling author of more than 300 books, audio, and video programs. He's the inventor of the patented InnerTalk technology and the founder and president of Progressive Awareness Research. He has been called a "master of the mind" and has appeared as an expert witness on both hypnosis and subliminal communication.

Eldon was a practicing criminalist conducting investigations and lie-detection examinations for many years. He is listed in more than a dozen Who's Who publications, including *Who's Who of Intellectuals* and *Who's Who in Science and Engineering*. He is a fellow in the American Psychotherapy Association and an internationally sought-after speaker. His books and audio-video materials have been translated into more than a dozen languages and have sold millions worldwide.

Eldon is the host of the popular radio show *Provocative Enlightenment.* He has interviewed some of the most interesting people on the planet. His shows are thought-provoking and always fresh in both their perspective and the exchange.

To Learn More about Eldon Taylor

If you've enjoyed this book and would like to learn more about tools to help you become the person you were meant to be, visit Eldon's website: **http://www.eldontaylor.com**.

If you're interested in gaining more control over your self-talk and your inner beliefs, you may wish to try Eldon's patented audio technology, InnerTalk. Independent researchers have repeatedly proven that InnerTalk is effective at changing thoughts and thereby influencing behavior in a variety of areas affecting daily life.

You may download free samples of InnerTalk and find a large selection of self-improvement products at **http://www.innertalk .com**.

To be informed about Eldon's latest research and work and to hear about special offers on Eldon's books and audio products, please subscribe to his free e-newsletter by going to **http://www .eldontaylor.com**. You may also request a free catalog by calling 1-800-964-3551 or writing to Progressive Awareness Research, Inc., PO Box 1139, Medical Lake, WA, 99022.

InnerTalk Distribution
USA
Progressive Awareness Research, Inc.
PO Box 1139
Medical Lake, WA 99022
U.S.A.
1-800-964-3551
1-509-299-3377
www.innertalk.com

U.K. and Ireland
Kiki Ltd.
Unit 4, Aylsham Business Estate
Shepheards Close,
Aylsham
Norfolk
NR11 6SZ
011 44 (0)1263 738 660
www.kiki-health.co.uk

Germany
Axent Verlag
Steinerne Furt 78
86167 Augsburg
Germany
011 49 821 70 5011
www.axent-verlag.de

Malaysia/Singapore/Brunei/Australia/
New Zealand/Papua New Guinea
InnerTalk Sdn Bhd
2–2 Jalan Pju 8/5E, Perdana Bus. Cntr.
Bandar Damansara Perdana,
47820 Petaling Jaya
Selangor, Malaysia
011 60 37 729 4745
www.innertalk-au.com
www.innertalk.com.my

Taiwan and China
Easy MindOpen
3F, No. 257, Ho-Ping East Rd. Sec. 2
Taipei, Taiwan, R.O.C.
011 886 (227) 010–468(1)
www.iamone.com.tw

Distribution Inquiries

For information about distributing InnerTalk programs, please contact:

Progressive Awareness Research, Inc.
PO Box 1139
Medical Lake, WA 99022
1-800-964-3551
1-509-299-3377
www.innertalk.com

NOTES

NOTES

NOTES

NOTES

NOTES

NOTES

HAY HOUSE TITLES OF RELATED INTEREST

YOU CAN HEAL YOUR LIFE, the movie,
starring Louise L. Hay & Friends
(available as a 1-DVD program and an expanded 2-DVD set)
Watch the trailer at: **www.LouiseHayMovie.com**

THE SHIFT, the movie,
starring Dr. Wayne W. Dyer
(available as a 1-DVD program and an expanded 2-DVD set)
Watch the trailer at: **www.DyerMovie.com**

GET OUT OF YOUR OWN WAY: Escape from Mind Traps,
by Tom Rusk, M.D.

SHIFT HAPPENS!: How to Live an Inspired Life . . . Starting Right Now!,
by Robert Holden, Ph.D.

*TRUTH, TRIUMPH, AND TRANSFORMATION: Sorting Out the Fact
from the Fiction in Universal Law,* by Sandra Anne Taylor

YOU CAN CREATE AN EXCEPTIONAL LIFE,
by Louise Hay and Cheryl Richardson

YOUR SOUL'S COMPASS: What Is Spiritual Guidance?,
by Joan Borysenko, Ph.D., and Gordon Dveirin, Ed.D.

All of the above are available at your local bookstore,
or may be ordered by contacting Hay House (see next page).

We hope you enjoyed this Hay House book.
If you'd like to receive our online catalog featuring
additional information on Hay House books and
products, or if you'd like to find out more about
the Hay Foundation, please contact:

Hay House, Inc., P.O. Box 5100, Carlsbad, CA 92018-5100
(760) 431-7695 or (800) 654-5126
(760) 431-6948 (fax) or (800) 650-5115 (fax)
www.hayhouse.com® • **www.hayfoundation.org**

Published and distributed in Australia by: Hay House Australia
Pty. Ltd., 18/36 Ralph St., Alexandria NSW 2015 • *Phone:* 612-9669-4299
Fax: 612-9669-4144 • www.hayhouse.com.au

Published and distributed in the United Kingdom by:
Hay House UK, Ltd., Astley House, 33 Notting Hill Gate, London W11 3JQ •
Phone: 44-20-3675-2450 • *Fax:* 44-20-3675-2451 • www.hayhouse.co.uk

Published and distributed in the Republic of South Africa by:
Hay House SA (Pty), Ltd., P.O. Box 990, Witkoppen 2068
Phone/Fax: 27-11-467-8904 • www.hayhouse.co.za

Published in India by: Hay House Publishers India, Muskaan Complex,
Plot No. 3, B-2, Vasant Kunj, New Delhi 110 070 • *Phone:* 91-11-4176-1620
Fax: 91-11-4176-1630 • www.hayhouse.co.in

Distributed in Canada by: Raincoast, 9050 Shaughnessy St.,
Vancouver, B.C. V6P 6E5 • *Phone:* (604) 323-7100
Fax: (604) 323-2600 • www.raincoast.com

Take Your Soul on a Vacation

Visit **www.HealYourLife.com**® to regroup, recharge,
and reconnect with your own magnificence. Featuring
blogs, mind-body-spirit news, and life-changing
wisdom from Louise Hay and friends.

Visit **www.HealYourLife.com** today!

Free e-newsletters from Hay House, the Ultimate Resource for Inspiration

Be the first to know about Hay House's dollar deals, free downloads, special offers, affirmation cards, giveaways, contests, and more!

 Get exclusive excerpts from our latest releases and videos from *Hay House Present Moments*.

 Enjoy uplifting personal stories, how-to articles, and healing advice, along with videos and empowering quotes, within *Heal Your Life*.

 Have an inspirational story to tell and a passion for writing? Sharpen your writing skills with insider tips from *Your Writing Life*.

Sign Up Now!

Get inspired, educate yourself, get a complimentary gift, and share the wisdom!

http://www.hayhouse.com/newsletters.php

Visit www.hayhouse.com to sign up today!

  HealYourLife.com ♥